Praise for *Designing Momentum*

"Before Brant's book, the only ogre I thought I knew was a green animated character. Turns out, I've confronted more ogres than I thought, and it's these critical pivot points in life that either sink us or redefine us. Brant's incredible personal story frames some real truths and practical applications that we can all use not just to survive but to *thrive* in seemingly unbearable conditions."

—Tom Webster
Partner, Sounds Profitable

"*Designing Momentum* is the book you need to overcome inertia and get the ball rolling in your life and work. From the most intimate changes in yourself to scalable changes in your organization, this book is full of insights, exercises, and inspiring stories that will get you moving. Of course, the most remarkable story of all is Brant's own story of re-creating momentum after life slammed on the brakes. This is a highly impactful book."

—Liane Davey, PhD
Bestselling Author of *The Good Fight*

"Waiting for the 'right moment' is the fastest way to fail. In *Designing Momentum*, Brant Menswar proves that success isn't about waiting—it's about creating the moments that move you forward."

—Tamsen Webster
Founder, Message Design Institute

"*Designing Momentum* is a transformative guide that captures the power of living moment-to-moment to overcome life's greatest challenges. Brant Menswar's deeply personal journey uniquely positions him to share this vital message."

—Nick Hutchison
Founder and CEO, BookThinkers, and Bestselling Author of *Rise of the Reader*

"Brant Menswar has crafted a brilliant blueprint for those seeking to harness the power of everyday moments. *Designing Momentum* is more than just a guide; it's a 'verbs-first' catalyst for personal and professional transformation. The practical strategies and real-life examples make it an invaluable resource for anyone committed to turning their goals into reality."

—Hank Norman
Co-founder, 2 Market Media, and Brand Builder

"The value of momentum is vastly underrated. With *Designing Momentum*, Brant Menswar provides a powerful framework for transforming everyday moments into extraordinary opportunities. His blend of personal stories and practical advice makes this book both inspiring and actionable. It's a must-have for anyone determined to create lasting momentum in their life."

—Steve Carlis
Co-founder, 2 Market Media

"*Designing Momentum* is a breakthrough guide for anyone feeling stuck or overwhelmed. Brant Menswar's powerful insights and actionable strategies help you harness the energy of everyday moments to build unstoppable momentum and achieve your goals. Whether you're navigating uncertainty, rediscovering hope, or creating a legacy, this book will inspire and empower you to make each moment count. Highly recommended!"

—**Erin King**
Creator of "The Energy Exam" and 2x Bestselling Author

"Pay attention to the implementable and intentional strategies in this book. Give yourself the luxury of making the most of the little moments to build big momentum. Approach this book with curiosity, and you will be delighted with the transformational approach to building an accountability plan that allows you to make a greater impact in the world."

—**Neen James**
Luxury Expert, Keynote Speaker, and Author of *Attention Pays*

"This essential guide for the twenty-first century reimagines mindfulness, patience, and focus, showing you how to apply them in transformative ways during every moment of your life. Along the way, Brant challenges harmful illusions and opens your eyes to the untapped power inside you—ready for the moment to burst forth. Do yourself a favor: get this book, dive in, and take notes. Go ahead and bump that ogre (you'll see). It's time to rediscover your purpose, reclaim your momentum, and redefine the rest of your life."

—**Noel Zamot**
Former Commander of the US Air Force's elite Test Pilot School,
a combat veteran, and the Author of the award-winning novels
The Archer's Thread and *The Feather's Push*

"Brant Menswar delivers a blueprint to navigate uncertainty, overcome challenges, and create a meaningful legacy. *Designing Momentum* fuels the journey to intentionality, fulfillment, and success, one moment at a time."

—**Kathleen Wood**
Founder and CEO, Kathleen Wood Partners

"My dear friend Brant has crafted something truly transformational. This profoundly personal journey of loss and redemption unveils a powerful testament to the resilience of the human spirit. This is not just another self-help book—it takes a revolutionary approach to success that goes beyond traditional thinking. This book demonstrates how intentionality can harness the power of everyday moments to create unstoppable momentum that becomes a life by design."

—**Amilya Antonetti**
Behaviorist and CEO, AMA Productions

DESIGNING
MOMENTUM

DESIGNING
MOMENTUM

A BIG GOAL BLUEPRINT FOR TRANSFORMING EVERYDAY MOMENTS INTO MASSIVE SUCCESS

BRANT MENSWAR

WILEY

Published by John Wiley & Sons, Inc., Hoboken, New Jersey.
Published simultaneously in Canada.

For general information on our other products and services or for technical support, please contact our Customer Care Department within the United States at (800) 762-2974, outside the United States at (317) 572-3993 or fax (317) 572-4002.

Wiley also publishes its books in a variety of electronic formats. Some content that appears in print may not be available in electronic formats. For more information about Wiley products, visit our web site at www.wiley.com.

Library of Congress Cataloging-in-Publication Data is available:

ISBN: 9781394330003 (cloth)
ISBN: 9781394330010 (ePub)
ISBN: 9781394330027 (ePDF)

Cover Design: Wiley
Cover Image: © wildpixel/Getty Images
Author Photo: © Guy Welch All rights owned by Brant Menswar
SKY10100160_031425

For Sherry. . .

So, so, so much.

I love you.

Contents

Introduction

LIFE SUCKS, THEN you die. That was my mantra not too long ago. I had suffered a devasting loss (which you will learn about in the first chapter) and found myself … stuck. Eh, that is letting myself off too easy. I had lost all hope and was going through the motions just to get to tomorrow. I had given up on achieving the level of success I wanted, never mind my crazy "dreams" of convincing millions of people that they were meant for more in this life. I found myself living in "survival mode," and I didn't know how to get out of it.

A single conversation with a dear friend changed everything (which you will learn about in the last chapter … wait, you have to read the whole book? Yes). I discovered the hidden power buried deep within living moment to moment. I learned to harness it and use it to not just get me "unstuck" but to restore my hope and build unstoppable momentum.

Why is it that the blur of activity surrounding your life most often leads you to become overworked, overanxious, and overwhelmed yet hardly ever leads you to become an overachiever?

You are "busy" but aren't making any real progress toward your big goals. You have tried every TikTok trend to move you closer to your dreams. You bought a daily planner to plot out your every move, you enrolled in that online course that promised to reveal the secrets of the uber-successful, and you purchased a gratitude journal to keep you positive and thankful for what you already have. Hell, you even bought a vibration plate to stand on and shake the shit out of all the negative energy your body is holding on to.

Nothing has worked. Yet.

Believe me, you are not alone in feeling this way. It's easy to get caught up in a cycle of "activity," where you sacrifice long-term success for urgent short-term demands. The problem is you are pursuing your big aspirations in the wrong way. Rather than getting distracted by the urgency of everyday moments, you should be using them to build the kind of momentum that moves you forward one moment at a time.

This book offers a practical blueprint for transforming ordinary moments into extraordinary opportunities for growth and success. In fact, this book was born out of a series of everyday moments.

Moment 1: The Unsolicited Email

On January 9, 2024, I received an unsolicited email from a guy named Maxwell, a business development manager who worked for a company called 2 Market Media (2MM). I had heard of them before as they were a driving force behind launching the brands of Mel Robbins, Grant Cardone, and Evan Carmichael, to name a few. Max said he found me through a podcast I had been a guest on and had done a deep dive into my content. He loved the level of care and passion I put into what I do and explained that they "hand-pick" people they think are "rising stars" that they want to work with—consider my ego sufficiently stroked. Max made me feel like I *belonged* in the conversation. He asked to set up a quick call to learn about my goals and to see if what 2MM does would be of help. If I'm being honest, I wasn't looking for any help with my branding at the time. But my curiosity and ego decided to set up a call and see what Max had to say.

Moment 2: The Discovery Call

Three days later, my wife Sherry and I jumped on a video call to learn more about 2MM, what they do, and how they work. Max answered all of our questions and had some of his own. He wanted to get a clear *understanding* of where our business was at and what we were trying to build. On the surface, it looked like there could be some synergy. I have long been an admirer of 2MM clients. They have built powerful brands that connect with millions of people but in very different ways. I had some questions as to how 2MM would determine which path was correct for me. Max offered to connect us with well-known media veteran, entertainment executive, and 2MM co-founder Steve Carlis.

Moment 3: The Transformational Moment

A week later, Sherry and I found ourselves on a video chat with Steve. Before we had a chance to get started, Steve told me he had done some research on me and wanted to extend his sympathies for the devastating loss I referred to earlier (sorry, you are still going to have to read Chapter 1). He then talked about his daughter and the intense health struggles she faced when she was born. Steve didn't just placate my feelings or say something because it was "the right thing to do." He opened his heart and spoke through authentic, broken words to create a palpable level of *meaning* and *purpose*. I connected on such a deep level that I would have said yes to just about anything he suggested. The funny thing is, having worked with Steve and the team for the better part of a year now, being vulnerable is not Steve's "thing"—this was just a truly powerful moment that ignited the incredible momentum we have been building together ever since.

What you don't yet realize is that this series of three simple, everyday moments contained all four of the elements needed to create momentum: a sense of belonging, understanding, meaning, and purpose. The momentum these moments created has birthed a brilliant idea, powerful message, strong brand, growing podcast, and this book.

Designing Momentum isn't just about theory; it's "verbs first." One of my favorite sessions with 2MM's other co-founder Hank Norman was a spirited exchange during a methodology call on how to present the information in this book. Every time Hank would ask me a direct question, I would begin to give context before I gave my answer. As Hank got increasingly frustrated with me, he finally leaned into his laptop screen and yelled at the top of his lungs, "VERBS FIRST!" We both laughed our asses off, but his point was received excruciatingly loud and clear.

This book will tell you exactly how to use moments to build momentum, in a verbs-first style. I mean, just read the table of contents! These are strategies that I have used successfully to lift myself to another level and generate enough momentum to convince my publisher that it actually works. If you take the time to learn from these strategies and do the work (aaaaaand do the work), I know they will work for you as well.

Designing Momentum is an invitation for you to become the architect of your own success. It's a call to action to reclaim your time, energy, and focus and to design a life filled with meaning, purpose, and unstoppable momentum.

It's time to create a future worth remembering, one moment at a time.

PART

I

The Context

1

Stop Ghosting Yourself: The High Cost of Mental Time Travel

Momentum Objectives:

- Recognize the dangers of fixating on your past and future.
- Reframe past experiences for a more balanced narrative.
- Battle the illusion of control with deliberate, intentional action.
- Understand the real cost of absence and the importance of being present.

YOUR MIND IS a mental time machine, allowing you to travel between different eras of your life. One moment, you are reliving a past mistake, replaying a painful memory, or wallowing over a missed opportunity. The next, you are projecting yourself into an imagined future, a land of make-believe, consumed with anxiety about potential failures and worrying about all the uncertainty that comes with the unknown. It is ... exhausting. In fact, the constant mental time travel is creating a burden so significant that it is stopping you from engaging in your life and, more important, from accessing the power within the present moment.

3

"Check out the big brain on Brad!" The infamous line from the cult classic film *Pulp Fiction* is a fun reminder that the human brain is indeed remarkable, and in the words of Samuel L. Jackson, we all have the capability to be "smart motherf*ckers." In fact, the brain's creativity and imagination mixed with the ability to project thoughts, feelings, and behaviors onto someone else isn't just impressive; it's potentially dangerous. The brain can trap you in a perpetual cycle of time travel that never lets you experience the present moment. You get pulled into the past, haunted by regrets and the dreaded "what ifs," while simultaneously being pushed into the future so you can worry about what hasn't happened yet.

Hear me say this: you are not Marty McFly. (That is a reference to the movie *Back to the Future*. ... I got you, Gen Z.) You are *not* a time traveler.

Loosening the Grip of the Past

Your past, with its Amazon-style warehouse of memories, can be tricky to navigate. It shapes who you think you are, influences your decisions, and provides a sense of how you got to where you are now. While some of these memories are bursting with joy and offer comfort when you need them, others become shackles that bind you to the scabbed-over wounds of the past. These truly painful memories can play on repeat, over and over, becoming energy vampires and preventing you from embracing the moment right in front of you. You become so hyperfocused on what *was* that you miss out on the potential of what *is*.

Did you know the human mind has a peculiar tendency to fixate on the negative? It's not just you. It's all of us. Our brains want to dig into the dirty details of past mistakes and shame us for what we should have done differently. This process of reflection, on the surface, appears to be driven by a desire for understanding or even self-improvement. However, it often becomes a self-destructive cycle that traps you in an endless loop of negative self-talk, crushing your self-esteem and ushering in a sense of overall ... well ... "sh*ttiness." Wait, was I supposed to spell that with a "y"? I could never get that right. You get the point.

This fixation on the past can manifest itself in a variety of ways. You might hold on to grudges a little longer or relive past hurts so tightly that they poison your current relationships. You might constantly compare your present situation to a false, romanticized version of your past, convincing yourself that life was simpler and you were happier. You might relive the "glory days" of your youth so often that you don't engage in the reality of your current life. You may even sabotage your own success by telling yourself that you are not smart enough, your best days are behind you, or you are not worthy of happiness.

The emotional toll of continuously looking over your shoulder can give you more than a stiff neck. It can suck the life out of you, making you feel exhausted and constantly depressed. It can trigger your anxiety and distort your view of the present moment so much that you miss the opportunity to experience true joy. And then come the physical problems: headaches, stomach issues, sexual dysfunction, lack of sleep, aches and pains, and to top it off, no motivation to want to deal with any of it. Sound familiar?

The truth is you become emotionally unavailable to pretty much everyone. You disconnect, banishing yourself to a private emotional island to play a sad solo version of *Survivor*. You miss the opportunities to create new memories because you have decided to put on your producer hat and splice together a TikTok-worthy reel of the worst moments of your life just so you can watch it on repeat.

Loosening the grip of the past requires deliberate intention. You need to recognize the patterns of negativity and rewrite the stories you tell yourself about your past experiences. However, it isn't always a pattern of negativity; sometimes it's an "illusion of negativity" that twists your memories and makes it hard to remember the "happy" stuff but easy to recall an embarrassing moment with vivid detail. The mere aura of negativity has the ability to consume your memory and distort your perspective. Whether a pattern or illusion, it requires amping up your ability for self-compassion and forgiving yourself for prior mistakes. It requires letting go. It's time to accept the fact that you can't change the past and you need to hand over the keys to your time machine.

Take a Moment

That's Not How I Remember It...

Let's reframe a past experience to reduce its emotional grip. Write down a painful or regretful memory that often invades your thoughts. What are the lessons learned from this experience, and how has it contributed to your growth? How does this new narrative make you feel about the memory?

It's important to point out that the process of letting go isn't about forgetting or denying the past. It's about reframing your experiences, both good and bad, into a more balanced narrative of your life. You can honor your past without being defined, fooled, manipulated, or controlled by it.

Reframing My Own Past

I know this intimately. In 2012 my eldest son, Theo, was diagnosed with a rare blood cancer called myelodysplastic syndrome that required a bone marrow transplant to survive. On August 12, 2012, Theo received his transplant and began a 263-day nightmare in the Kids Beating Cancer Pediatric Transplant Center at Florida Hospital in Orlando.

While the transplant was successful, Theo developed a horrendous case of graft-versus-host disease, or GVHD, which happens when the donated bone marrow doesn't recognize the transplant environment and begins to attack the body. The only treatment when this happens is to suppress the immune system and hope for the best. If you reach level 4 of GVHD, it's fatal. Theo had reached that level and was seemingly going for a world record. Unfortunately, this treatment places the body at extreme risk of infection. As fate would have it, he contracted a deadly fungus called mucormycosis. The proper treatment for this infection is to radically boost the immune system so the body can attack the fungus. Two necessary treatments with opposite tactics created a zero-sum game. On March 23, 2013, the team of doctors called me into a room and explained that no matter which issue they treated, the other would take Theo's life. They recommended that I call who I needed to and go back to my son's hospital room and say my goodbyes.

I was living my real-life nightmare, and I couldn't wake myself up from it. I walked back to the room desperately trying to think about what to say and how to explain this to Theo's younger brother, Brady. As I sat on the edge of Theo's bed, I gave away every ounce of hope I had based on the recommendation of a room full of doctors. I didn't want to. I knew they didn't have the kind of power to determine who lives and dies. But I did it anyway. And instead of fighting for a miracle, I made the worst decision I have ever made. Against my better judgement, I said goodbye.

Hearing your child quietly whisper "I'm going to miss you, Daddy" is something you don't get over. Ever.

But meanwhile, something miraculous was happening. When I called my younger brother, Todd, to tell him the dire news, he was devastated. To make matters worse, he lived 1,500 miles away and couldn't make it to the hospital in time. So instead, he threw a Hail Mary. He filmed a video of himself holding up 55 different posterboards explaining Theo's case and pleading for help from anyone who could. He never actually said a word in the video. He only played the song "Fix You" by Coldplay as the soundtrack for a desperately needed miracle.

Almost overnight, the video had 500,000 views. We started to receive calls from people all over the world who believed they could help. The callers included brilliant doctors with uniquely specific experience in the challenges we were facing. Come to find out, the zero-sum game our doctors perceived wasn't entirely true. An experimental treatment would allow us to address both diseases at the same time—an option our doctors hadn't been unaware of. Within 24 hours of my brother's video going viral, we had a crazy plan to try to save Theo's life.

It worked.

Theo's body began to recover, and after a few more months in the hospital, he was able to come home. I couldn't foresee the fairytale outcome of my living nightmare. In the moment the doctors suggested to say my goodbyes, my feelings suffocated any other possible option. Sometimes your feelings don't leave room for fairytales.

Those desolate moments can breed the worst decisions. Relying solely on your scattered emotions rather than your non-negotiable values to make important decisions is a recipe for regret. When your emotions run hot, there is a real danger of saying things you don't mean and overreacting to things in order to "protect" yourself from danger. You place any positive impact you hoped for at risk when you don't ground yourself in the things that matter most to you.

My memory of sitting on the edge of Theo's bed and saying goodbye has been the cause of many sleepless nights in the years since.

The question inside my head plays over and over in an endless loop: *I wonder if he thinks I gave up on him.* I beat myself up for years over this. I couldn't celebrate the reality of the moment because I was trapped in the past.

I decided to figure out what my true non-negotiable values were so that if I ever found myself in a similar situation, I would know exactly what to say and how to approach it. Creativity, hope, impact, empathy, authenticity, and family are the values that now guide my actions. Every decision I have made since discovering them has been filtered through these six things. Living with this deliberate intention has transformed my life so greatly that I even wrote a book about it in 2020 called *Black Sheep: Unleash the Extraordinary, Awe-Inspiring, Undiscovered You* to help others discover their core values and start living a life of deliberate intention.

Unfortunately, I was given another chance in 2021. Sometimes, the treatment is worse than the disease. Theo's body had taken an awful toll over the nine years he battled. While his mind was as strong and witty as ever, his body was weak—too weak to withstand a global pandemic. In early 2021, Theo contracted COVID-19, and I soon found myself sitting on the edge of his hospital bed, having to have the same conversation I did years earlier. This time, I purposefully didn't say my goodbyes. Instead, I spoke my values into existence. Even though Theo was intubated and in a medically induced coma, I talked to him about the creative things he loved to do. I told him I wouldn't give up hope. I spoke about all the people he had impacted and how it had changed their faith and view of what's possible. I also told him how proud I was of him for fighting, and if he felt like he was too tired to fight anymore, I understood and would support him in whatever he chose.

On February 27, 2021, Theo lost his battle.

Having suffered an immeasurable loss, it would be easy to cover myself with the blanket of suffering and find others to lament with. For a while, I did just that. But how is that honoring my past? It isn't. You can choose to move forward to the present moment and cherish the memories that helped mold you into the human you are today. It isn't easy, but it is necessary if you want to create the type of momentum that has legacy-worthy impact.

You are not your past mistakes or wounds. You are wholly human, and though you are filled with the scars of your unique experiences, you have the power to decide what will shape your present and future. You decide what to let go of and when to open yourself up to new opportunities, relationships, and possibilities.

Don't allow your past to imprison you. You hold the keys to unlock a future worth living for.

Future Fantasy: The Illusion of Control

When you think about the future, the anxiety that tags along stems from the desire to control everything. I am a self-professed, card-carrying diamond club member of Control Freaks Anonymous. If you invited me to dinner, I would say yes and then drive *your* car to get us there. I need control, or at least the feeling of control. That can be a problem. Let me rephrase that: that is often a problem.

Here's the thing: the human brain craves certainty. This need can become dangerously obsessive, especially when living in a world where uncertainty is the only constant. Your brain will do anything, even lie to you, to satisfy the need for a sense of believable certainty. Your brain wants to avoid pain at any cost, so it will have you try to predict and plan for every possible outcome to avoid getting hurt. You become seduced by the illusion of control, but the uncertainty only amplifies your anxieties and pulls you out of the present moment.

Your anxiety about the future is all about fear: fear of failure, fear of the unknown, or even fear of loss. Because of this, you try to meticulously plan every detail to mitigate your fears. You create contingency plans to account for every possible scenario, hoping to preempt any potential setbacks. This can manifest itself as:

- **Olympic-level worrying:** You become obsessed with what "could" happen, worrying about all the "bad stuff" that is potentially lurking around the corner. You deplete your emotional reserves and become increasingly unstable. You begin to remove yourself from the present moment, lost in a world that hasn't happened yet.
- **Obsessive list-making:** You begin to make lists for everything: groceries, to-dos, worries, problems ... hell, you make lists of lists! This is your way to avoid engaging in the present moment. You document every detail so you don't have to take any action, simply adding to the lists continuously. While you tell yourself you are getting "organized," you really are paralyzing yourself.
- **Strict schedules or routines:** You create rigid schedules and routines to try to control your environment. You become increasingly inflexible and refuse to adapt to change, causing you to become more anxious when things don't go according to plan. You become so focused on sticking to the schedule that you miss the moment happening right in front of you.

All of these create a feeling of control to give you a temporary sense of comfort, but in reality, they provide a false sense of security in a chaotic and unpredictable world. It makes you believe that you are in the driver's seat, following your GPS to your destination. But it's not real. In fact, it is a fragile perception that can be shattered by the smallest of pebbles kicked up by unforeseen circumstances or unexpected challenges leaving you feeling overwhelmed and helpless.

The irony is the more you "think" you have control, the less you actually do. The obsession over what might be pulls you from engaging in the moment at hand. You become so focused on alleviating potential problems in the future that you miss all of the opportunities right in front of you. You once again become a prisoner, this time of your own anxieties.

Taking up residence in the future disconnects you from the only place you can affect change—the present moment. It's here where you make the decisions that will influence the course of your life. When you tie yourself up with the chains of the future, you forfeit the power to actually change it. You become a timid hitchhiker afraid to stick your thumb out and move toward your goals.

Letting go of the illusion of control isn't about abandoning your plans or leaving it up to fate. It's about recognizing the importance of deliberate intention and making the best decisions possible in the present. These are decisions that are rooted in your core values; consider all the facts and honor your feelings in the moment. This is the best you can do because the truth is you can't control outcomes. You can only control the deliberate intention that goes into making a decision.

If you want to influence your future, it starts in the present. This is where you will learn to navigate change and overcome unexpected challenges with resilience and grace. You will learn to appreciate the present for what it truly is: a fleeting moment waiting to be captured and embraced.

Take a Moment

Tear It Up

Let's reduce your anxiety about the future by recognizing and releasing the need for control. Identify a current situation where you feel a strong need to control the outcome.

Take a piece of paper and draw a vertical line down the middle. On the left side, list the aspects of the situation that are within your control, and on the right side, list those that are not. Focusing on the left side, write down several ideas on how to approach the things that are within your control. Cut the paper down the middle vertical line. Take the right side of things that are out of your control and tear it to pieces. This exercise is a powerful way to signify that you can let these things go.

The High Cost of Absence

When you are living your life like *Bill & Ted's Excellent Adventure*, trapped in mental time travel (another 1980s movie, Gen Z—it might be a good idea to take notes), you end up paying a steep price: the cost of absence. Absent from your own life. Absent from harnessing the power of the present moment and all it has to offer. You ultimately end up ghosting yourself.

If you stopped reading for a moment and just listened, what would you hear? Is it a bird chirping, your children laughing, rain falling on the roof, church bells ringing, or your dog snoring? It's these subtle wonders and simple joys that are the very essence of the present moment. When you are absent from your own life, you miss these everyday miracles.

How are your relationships at the moment? Do your loved ones feel seen and supported? When you are hyperfocused on only your issues, you become impatient and less empathetic. You stop truly listening and nurturing even your closest connections. This is one of the worst side effects of being emotionally unavailable. At some point, it is imperative that you address the improper illusions that you carry around in your mind, as they have a very real impact on those around you. Reframing your illusions is not just about being in the moment; it's often the best thing you can do for your relationships with loved ones.

Do you consider yourself a creative? Having your mind clouded with worries and anxiety makes it nearly impossible to be creative or productive. Your concentration will wane, your motivation will dwindle, and your ability to generate new ideas will diminish. The romanticizing of being a frustrated artist or musician is a toxic thought. It doesn't have to be that way. Everything you need to pull yourself out of creative constipation is in the present moment.

Ultimately, being absent can disconnect you from your physical self. You find yourself gaining weight, eating poorly, not exercising, and missing the signals your body is trying to send you to stop ignoring your well-being. You get used to the tension in your neck, the tiredness, and the general feeling of blah.

Can we make a deal right now? If you agree to hand over the keys to the mental time machine, I will give you a simple four-step process to capture the power of the present moment and catapult yourself toward achieving your biggest goals.

Deal? Deal.

Moments to Remember:
- Your brain can trap you in a perpetual cycle of time travel that never lets you experience the present moment.
- The human mind has a peculiar tendency to fixate on the negative.
- Your brain will do anything, including lie to you, to satisfy its need for certainty.
- Loosening the grip of the past requires recognizing the patterns and illusions of negativity and reframing the stories you tell yourself about your past experiences.
- You are not your past mistakes or wounds.
- The illusion of control over your future gives you a temporary sense of comfort but a false sense of security.
- Being absent from the present moment can disconnect you from your physical self.

2

Capture the Moment: How Everyday Moments Can Create Unstoppable Momentum

Momentum Objectives:

- Discard the myth of a "big moment" mindset.
- Learn to recognize and capture the potential within everyday moments.
- Repurpose your "survival mode" instincts to capitalize on present moments.
- Empower yourself to "own a moment" through Moment Momentum.

SOME PEOPLE BELIEVE that momentum is generated on the back of a single huge success, that it takes a big moment to kickstart momentum. When you look at pop culture, it often seems that some of your favorite actors, celebrities, and musicians just popped up on the radar screen after a red-carpet event or concert and had immediate overnight success. This "big moment" belief is a myth.

During the 2011 Grammy Awards, a "new" band by the name of Mumford and Sons was performing their song "The Cave" as part of a special tribute to acoustic music alongside Bob Dylan, the Avett Brothers, Stu Kimball, Donnie Herron, and Tony Garnier. This is the "moment" everyone attributes to Mumford and Sons' explosion onto the U.S. music scene. But the truth is that Mumford and Sons had been touring relentlessly for four years before this ceremony took place. They were gathering fans one show at a time, treating every moment like it was the only time they would ever get a chance to play. They were building momentum song by song. Their passion and ability to focus on and own these moments are what was stacking people thousands deep at their concerts and gathering fans in droves. The "overnight" Grammy success was a mirage.

Thinking you need some massive win or once-in-a-lifetime, earth-shattering event to set the wheels of momentum in motion is simply … bullsh*t. The problem isn't a lack of big moments; it's a failure to recognize and capture the small ones. Real momentum, the kind that can alter your future, is captured one marginal moment at a time.

Your life is not an Instagram highlight reel. It's a big, beautiful, chaotic, messy collection of everyday moments: the frantic dash to get the kids fed, dressed, and off to school; the hectic commute to work; the quick stop at Dunkin' for coffee (sorry, Starbucks); and the awkward quiet ride in the elevator at work. These seemingly insignificant moments are all filled with potential momentum. When you realize that literally a single moment can change the rest of your life, there is a sense of urgency to find and capture that moment. It's incredibly exciting.

What stops a lot of us from building momentum is having a "big moment" mindset, where you feel like without a massive moment to springboard yourself, you will never build the momentum you need to reach your goals. So you either wait for the big moment to happen or simply stop pushing.

Let's change that perspective. When you look at your life as a series of moments, you realize that if you miss one particular moment, there's going to be another one. If you can start to live your life moment to moment, you can begin to unlock the power held within each moment. You never know which one will push things forward and start the momentum you need.

Take a Moment

An Insignificant Surprise

Write down one seemingly insignificant moment that had a positive impact on your day. Was it a quick exchange with a co-worker? Was it grabbing your morning coffee at the local coffee shop? Why was this moment meaningful?

Repurposing Survival Mode

The idea of living your life moment to moment might be scary, but I would bet you have already experienced living this way at some point in your life. You might refer to it as "survival mode." This state of being is your natural human response to stressful situations. It moves your brain and body into a state of high alert and prioritizes your safety above everything else. When you enter survival mode, your brain pumps adrenaline and cortisol into your system to try to get you ready both physically and mentally to deal with a perceived threat. You feel your heart beat faster, your breathing changes, your muscles tighten up, and all of your senses are heightened. It is then that you have to choose a survival response.

The four survival response choices are *fight*, *flight*, *freeze*, and *fawn*. You can toe up and face a moment, but approaching it as a fight doesn't put you in the best mindset. You can flee and run away, but that isn't going to move you forward. You might simply freeze during stressful situations and not do anything, or you might fawn and try to diffuse the situation with people-pleasing or submissive behavior.

I believe you can learn to repurpose survival mode and use it to capture those fleeting moments that can create the momentum you need to crush your goals. Survival mode forces you to deal only with the moment you are in and not on the potential challenges that lie ahead. You can take some of the benefits from being in a state of high alert, like using your heightened senses, to recognize a moment when it's upon you. If you are truly going to take advantage of this strategy, you need to add a fifth "F" word to consider: *focus*.

When you consciously choose to focus, you interrupt the automatic survival instinct. Instead of reacting with fear or paralysis, you shift into a state of mindful awareness. You pick up on subtle cues and insights that you might otherwise miss. Focus acts as a lens, directing your mental and emotional energy toward a specific point. This concentration enhances your problem-solving abilities, empowers you to make deliberate decisions, and fuels your momentum.

When you learn to adapt to life's uncertainty with focus, each step forward becomes part of a larger journey, fueling what I like to call *Moment Momentum*. This isn't just about bouncing back; it's about bouncing forward—turning every challenge into an opportunity to accelerate your personal and professional growth. You will learn to recognize that the same instincts that help you confront life's immediate challenges can be harnessed to propel you forward in meaningful ways. By exploring the intersection of survival, adaptability, and resilience, you will discover how these traits are not just reactive tools but proactive strategies for growth.

Moment Momentum

Welcome to the heart of your journey in this book: understanding Moment Momentum. How can this simple concept revolutionize the way you navigate your life, both personally and professionally? As you delve deeper into these pages, you'll discover the remarkable power of the present moment and how, with a shift in perspective, you can transform everyday moments into extraordinary momentum.

In the realm of physics, momentum is defined as the product of an object's mass and velocity, a force that propels an object forward. In life, momentum functions similarly; it's the force that propels you forward, the driving energy that moves you from where you are to where you want to be. But unlike physical momentum, life's momentum is not driven by mass and velocity, but by your actions and decisions.

Think about that for a minute. In your life, each decision you make and each action you take contribute to your life's momentum. Every step you take, no matter how small, either moves you closer to your goals or farther away. The concept of Moment Momentum, then, is about understanding and capitalizing on the opportunities that exist in every single moment to generate momentum. It is about using these moments as the foundation for the kind of upward movement and energy that can help push you toward your goal. If you take your goal and break it down into a series of immediate, achievable steps, you can also take each moment and use it as a tiny little turbo boost to keep you on your path.

Consider the example of British cycling coach Sir Dave Brails-
ford, who led the British cycling team to victory in the Tour de
France six times over seven years. His philosophy—the "aggrega-
tion of marginal goals"—was simple: it was about seeking a 1%
improvement in everything the team did. Small, incremental
gains, when added together, created a significant improvement
in overall performance and ultimately led to victories in 2012,
2013, 2015, 2016, 2017, and 2018.

This is the essence of Moment Momentum. It's about breaking
down your big, intimidating goals into manageable actions that
can be accomplished by owning moments and using each of them
to drive yourself forward. Remember:

Every moment counts, and every decision matters.

Have you ever played one of those "coin pusher" games at an
arcade or casino? The goal is to strategically drop quarters so they
land and push other quarters forward, ultimately pushing them
off the edge and into the payout slot. This is how Moment
Momentum works. Every time you own a moment, it's like dropping a quarter into the game. The more moments you own, the
better chance you give yourself that one of them is going to push
everything forward, allowing you to reap your reward.

Take a Moment

1% More

What is one small moment you could own to push you 1%
closer to achieving your goal? Schedule a time in your
calendar to complete that moment.

Big Goal Buy-In

Corporations and leaders can use Moment Momentum when trying to get buy-in from the front lines for the company's big goal. One of the hardest things to accomplish is to get the people far removed from the boardroom to take ownership of a company-wide initiative. While they might know what the big goal is, what can hourly workers really do that will help the company reach that 15% increase in market penetration? Is there something they can do that gives them the feeling that makes them believe their efforts matter? Yes.

They can *own a moment*. Empowering them to own a moment gives them accountability, a sense of belonging, and a feeling that their contribution truly matters. This is how you connect individual contributions to the larger objective. It takes a detached, overwhelming grand plan with unrelatable goals and makes it personal.

A "Foodie" Conversion

Matt Winn is the chief development officer for Maple Hospitality Group (MHG). My wife and I were introduced to Matt at an event we were both speaking at in Miami, Florida. MHG owns the infinitely popular restaurant chain Maple & Ash. My wife got onto Matt for not being able to get a table at their Chicago location for years during an annual industry event held at The Mart, the world's largest commercial building and design center. Matt laughed and told her he would personally make sure that wouldn't happen again. Several months later, Matt and I were speaking at another event together in Arizona, and he invited my wife and I and a small group of others to dine at Maple & Ash's Scottsdale location.

First let me say this, I am not a foodie. I eat so I won't die and would be happy having Fluffernutter sandwiches till I can't eat solid food anymore. But I can and do appreciate "an experience." That is the best way to describe eating at Maple & Ash. As soon as we stepped into the dining room, illuminated by Edison bulbs, we were transported on a culinary journey. With its esteemed menu crafted by two-Michelin-star chef Danny Grant and the intriguingly risqué artwork adorning the walls, all thoughts of Fluffernutters vanished from my mind.

Matt told us that MHG empowers and encourages their team to create an experience for everyone who dines with them. That translates to every server getting their own business cards. The next time you want to dine at Maple & Ash, you don't call the restaurant, you call your server, who will make you a reservation, greet you by name when you arrive, and personally serve your meal. Talk about empowering your people to own a moment!

MHG even carries their approach through to their recruiting, where they state, "We're a team that doesn't just work well together; we celebrate hard together too. We're looking for people who share our philosophy of generosity and fun, who love to take the initiative, and who never say no to making a moment unforgettable."

They look for "Moment Makers." In their words, "We don't miss an opportunity to make a memory worth returning to—we create experiences that surprise and delight. Whether or not it's a birthday, anniversary, or party, we don't need a reason to take our guests over the top with unexpected moments around every corner."

No wonder the front page of their website declares: "Work with the Best F@*king Restaurant Group We Know … and we know a lot." By giving everyone the power to own a moment, MHG is experiencing exponential growth. The big goals get achieved through the small moments.

Matt Winn is slowly trying to convert me to a foodie. If he keeps feeding me incredible meals that have me making provocatively inappropriate noises due to the deliciousness, I just may put my Fluffernutter down ... for a moment.

"People First" Personified

When you experience an employee owning a moment, a memorable connection is created that often leads to brand loyalty. Last year, our youngest son was driving alone to a hockey camp in Canada from Colorado. He had been driving for almost 12 hours and was getting desperately tired. It was getting late, and he was struggling to reserve a room as the options were limited, and he was only 20 years old. My wife began to call the hotels along the route to see if they would allow us to rent the room in his name. The first two hotels simply denied our request, but the third call was answered by an empowered employee of a Marriott hotel who happened to be a mom and understood my wife's growing panic. She had us sign the necessary paperwork and allowed us to reserve the room, but then she did something incredible.

When our son arrived at nearly midnight, along with his room key, she had put together some food for him as he hadn't had a chance to find a place to eat. She made sure he was comfortable and even made him a box of snacks for his ride the next day. *This is owning a moment.*

I would venture to guess that this sweet, kind woman doesn't wake up each morning and begin to map out her contribution toward Marriott's big goals. But by owning a moment and taking extraordinary care of our son, we have become diehard brand ambassadors! Not only do we now stay exclusively at Marriott properties when we travel, but I have told this story on stage to tens of thousands of people at conferences. Her single act of owning a moment has now been amplified through my endless recanting of this story. Who knows how many people sitting in one of my audiences have decided to stay at a Marriott property because of this woman's "moment."

Take a Moment

Moment Makers

What are three ways you could empower someone on your team to "own a moment"? How will you show your team that their efforts matter? In what ways are you empowering your people to step up?

According to our research at Black Sheep Foundry over the past four years, the most frustrating position for an employee to be in is to have "responsibility without authority." Being held responsible for meeting a client's needs without the authority to make any decisions is not empowering anyone to own a moment. In fact, it's doing just the opposite; your people will be missing opportunities to create the momentum your organization needs to hit those big goals.

In subsequent chapters, we will go deeper into the practical aspects of Moment Momentum, exploring how you can apply this concept to various aspects of your life at work and at home. We will discuss strategies for capturing a moment, building and amplifying momentum, and overcoming challenges along the way.

Moments to Remember:

- A "big moment" mindset can stop momentum.
- Real momentum, the kind that can alter your future, is captured one marginal moment at a time.
- The fifth survival response is *focus*. When you consciously choose to focus, you interrupt the automatic survival instinct.
- Moment Momentum is about understanding and capitalizing on the opportunities that exist in every moment.
- Empowering people to own a moment gives them accountability, a sense of belonging, and a feeling that their contribution truly matters.

3

Unravel the Five-Year Plan: Unlocking the Power of Uncertainty

Momentum Objectives:

- Understand how five-year plans have their limitations in the face of uncertainty.
- Recognize how uncertainty can be a powerful ally in achieving long-term goals.
- Learn the importance of pivoting in adapting to change.
- Discover how to find order within the chaos.

FIVE-YEAR PLANS. Remember when your school counselor recommended those? They are intended to give you a sense of security, a roadmap you can follow to the future. But if we are being honest, how often do they actually pan out the way you planned? As the saying goes, sh*t happens. The world changes, your life goes sideways, and your five-year plan gets rendered moot in the blink of an eye. Trying to hold on to something so rigid can actually handcuff you from finding the success you're looking for. You need to be much more adaptable, ready to pivot on a moment's notice.

While uncertainty is often perceived as the enemy of progress, it can be our most powerful ally. It's in the constant required pivots, being forced to function in *moments*, where the true power of uncertainty resides.

It's like trying to follow your Global Positioning System (GPS) while driving. You can enter your destination and allow the GPS to set your course. But as you begin your journey, circumstances can change. Accidents happen, road construction slows down progress, and bad weather can creep in and change your course. What happens when your GPS experiences these obstacles? It offers you suggestions to reroute. You can stay on the course that was originally set, but it's going to take you longer to get to your destination. Chances are, you are going to let some birds and words fly as your frustration builds and your time is wasted. But you don't have to make that choice. You could simply allow your GPS to reroute you on a faster, less stressful path to where you want to go. This power of uncertainty allows you to make last-minute changes to stay on track.

Now listen, I'm not suggesting that you completely abandon your long-term plans. That would be ridiculous. I am suggesting you change your approach to achieving those goals. We all need long-term plans to give us something to shoot for. It's important to dream. It's important to stretch toward goals that might seem slightly out of reach. I just want you to have the best possible chance of actually achieving those goals, and that requires a change in your methods.

Embracing uncertainty doesn't mean being reckless or unprepared. It means being open to new possibilities, being willing to adapt, and trusting your ability to navigate whatever comes your way. It means recognizing that the unexpected can often lead to the most rewarding experiences.

When Harold Mantius began working as an engineer for Ocean Spray, he was given a tour around the plant. Ocean Spray, the world's largest producer of cranberry juice, is a cooperative founded nearly 100 years ago and owned by 700 different families. While on the tour, he noticed an enormous amount (literally tons) of cranberry hulls being discarded. This outer skin was a byproduct of extracting the juice from the cranberry and was collected and sold as cattle feed for pennies on the dollar. Mantius knew there had to be something else that could be done with these hulls to make them more profitable. So he took it upon himself to do some experimenting. He realized that he could process the hulls, reinject them with a little leftover juice, and *voilà* … the Craisin® was born. This unexpected discovery has become so popular that there is now an overage of cranberry juice due to the amount of extraction needed to create the Craisin! Ever wonder why you can buy juice blends like Cran-Orange, Cran-Apple, and Cran-Grape? You can thank Harold for that. By being open to the possibilities and embracing uncertainty, he created an entirely new market segment that has catapulted Ocean Spray to a nearly $2 billion company.

When you're open to the unknown, you're more likely to see opportunities that others miss. You're more willing to take calculated risks, to step outside your comfort zone, and to discover new paths to success.

Take a Moment

Unusual Solutions

Identify one current personal or professional challenge. Set a timer for five minutes and brainstorm as many unusual or unexpected solutions as possible.

"Pivot, Pivaat, Pivaaaat!": When Uncertainty Breeds Success

Like the classic episode of *Friends* where Ross keeps yelling, "Pivot," at Chandler and Rachel while carrying a sofa up a flight of stairs, there are times when we need to shift direction to find success.

The ability to pivot is a crucial skill for navigating life's ups and downs. It's about recognizing when the initial plan isn't working and having the courage to try something different. Pivoting isn't simply reacting to change; it's about grabbing change by the horns and riding it toward new opportunities to achieve something greater than what you thought possible.

I am reminded of the classic scene in the *Blues Brothers* movie when Jake and Elwood are attempting to play their Motown-style blues in Bob's Country Bunker, a honkey-tonk bar in Kokomo, Indiana. They quickly come to the realization, from the beer bottles being launched like missiles at the chicken wire surrounding them, that this type of music wasn't going to work. They recognize the moment and immediately pivot to playing the only country song they know, the theme song from the TV show *Rawhide*, to the delight of drunken cowboys everywhere.

The true strength of a pivot is in understanding that change is not just probable; it's inevitable. If you are going to accept the fact that it is not if change is going to come but rather when change will come, you also have to accept that uncertainty is riding shotgun. Uncertainty and change are inseparable travel buddies. You can choose to embrace their arrival or try to ignore them and inevitably find them sprawled out camping on your front lawn. The faster you welcome them, the quicker you discover new opportunities that weren't available before they showed up.

Most of us are familiar with Instagram, but did you know it started as Burbn, a location-based check-in app? Founders Kevin Systrom and Mike Krieger were struggling to acquire users as the app was too cumbersome. When looking over the data, they noticed their users were most engaged when simply sharing photos. They quickly embraced the change and uncertainty, pivoted drastically, and gained more than a million users in the first month of launching Instagram. A year later, they were at 10 million users. Fast-forward a decade or so, and the founders sold the platform to Mark Zuckerberg for a cool $1 billion.

The power of a good pivot is found in a complete transformation of your perspective. It's when you understand that the setbacks you are going to face aren't actually failures; they're informants! Setbacks can give you the crucial information you need to overcome the obstacles you face and build the momentum you desire.

When you find the courage to embrace the unexpected and begin to recognize the potential hidden in the unknown, you start on the path to a more authentic and meaningful life. You become more resilient in the face of adversity and find yourself adopting a growth mindset.

This perspective shift is a fundamental change in how you view the world and your place within it. It's a move away from feeling weak, where challenges are seen as threats to your abilities, to feeling strong and empowered, where challenges are seen as opportunities for personal development. Let me say this: it's not simply the power of positive thinking (although there is some merit to that). This is a conscious and deliberate reframing of your experiences. It's looking at things as happening *for* you and not *to* you, even in the most difficult scenarios.

I used to hate that saying, especially in the reality of losing my son. But the truth is, without those horrendous experiences, I never would have discovered what my non-negotiable values are. I never would have written my first book. I wouldn't have helped tens of thousands of people discover what matters most to them, and I certainly wouldn't be writing this book as you read it. In fact, I don't know that I would be desperately fighting for a legacy worth remembering without facing those struggles, as much as I wish I hadn't had to. The unknown can be a relentless source of anxiety and fear, but it can also be a source of immense opportunity if you have the balls (pardon the reference, ladies) to accept the adventure.

Take a Moment

Got Some Change?

For one day, jot down every time plans, even small ones, change. What was your initial reaction? How did you pivot the change?

Recalibrating Success

Pivoting often requires redefining success itself. Big goals, particularly in Western cultures, are frequently driven by external metrics like financial gain, social status, or specific milestones—the corner office, the six-figure salary, the 1971 matte black Corvette convertible (okay, that's mine), or the perfect Olan Mills family portrait (you know you have one). These traditional markers of success are only a shallow understanding of what truly brings fulfillment. They are often imposed by societal expectations and social media influencers hocking their $49 online courses, rather than arising from our intrinsic non-negotiable values.

The process of adapting to change, however, can disrupt your pursuit of what you define as success. When faced with heavy, real-life challenges like losing a loved one or going through a difficult divorce, the pursuit of the fancy car or the powerful promotion can feel meaningless. I think we all faced this idea during the pandemic. It forced us to confront deeper questions about what truly gives our lives purpose and meaning.

This disruption can be a catalyst for profound introspection. You begin to examine the underlying motivations that drive your choices. Are you chasing a definition of success imposed on you, or are you pursuing goals aligned with what matters most to you? This self-examination can lead to a shift in priorities and a recalibration of what constitutes a meaningful life.

This recalibration of success often manifests as a move away from external validation toward intrinsic values. Personal fulfillment becomes more important than social status. Meaningful relationships take precedence over material possessions. Contributing to a greater purpose, whether through service to others or pursuing a passion, becomes the new benchmark for achievement.

This shift doesn't mean you have to abandon your previously held goals. It's about reevaluating them through a new lens, a lens informed by a deeper understanding of your values. Financial security, for example, might still be a goal, but it's pursued not as an end in itself, but as a means to support a life aligned with your values—perhaps providing for your loved ones, enabling you to pursue creative endeavors, or contributing to causes you believe in.

This recalibrated definition of success allows for a more holistic and fulfilling experience. The outward appearance of achievement might differ from the initial vision. The corner office might be replaced by a home office, the six-figure salary by a modest income that supports a passion project, the perfect Olan Mills family portrait by a ... who are you kidding—it doesn't get any better. But the sense of fulfillment, the feeling of living a life aligned with your values, far surpasses the fleeting satisfaction of achieving what someone else deems successful. It's a success that redefines who you are, what you want, and why you want it.

Take a Moment

How Do You Spell Success?

Ignoring traditional metrics, define success in five words or less.

Finding Order in the Chaos

Uncertainty can feel chaotic, overwhelming even. But within that chaos lies the potential for growth, for innovation, for discovering new strengths and capabilities. It's in those moments when we're forced to find order in the wreckage of disorder that we truly evolve. Embracing uncertainty means learning to get comfortable with being uncomfortable. It's trusting that even in the throes of chaos, you can still find your way forward. Finding a path through the unknown simply means discovering ways to manage uncertainty. This can be anything from a major personal change like starting a new career to a societal shift like adapting to new technology, or even something as simple as figuring out a new route to work when your usual road is closed. It's about finding your footing in unfamiliar territory and creating a sense of stability amid all the change.

Here are some ways to find order in the chaos:

- **Create routines and rituals:** When the world feels like it's crumbling around you and you have no control over what's happening, being able to settle into your routines and rituals can be incredibly comforting. This does not mean you don't venture out into the unknown; it means you throw down some anchors that make you feel safe and connected to reality.
- **Focus on what you *can* control:** In the midst of chaos, it's easy to become overwhelmed by all the stuff you *can't* control.

So instead, focus your attention on the things you have absolute control over: things like what you say yes and no to, the way you respond to a challenging situation, or the inner monologue you recite to yourself. By doubling down on the things that are within your control, you can create a sense of order within the chaos.

- **Find connection and support:** Uncertainty is really good at making you feel like you are alone and that no one cares about what you are going through. It's when you feel like this that you need to reach out to friends and family to build a sense of community and shared experience. It's only through connection that someone can help share the burden you are carrying by giving you valuable insights, emotional support, and hope. It's connection that stabilizes your mindset and helps you find your footing.
- **Schedule some self-discovery time:** When you are staring down unexpected challenges, you are often forced to confront your own limitations and discover whatever hidden strengths you possess. You may discover that you're not as strong as you thought you were or that your carefully honed skills simply aren't good enough for the task at hand. This confrontation that you didn't ask for can smack you around, humble you, and shatter any illusion of control while exposing your vulnerabilities like an atomic wedgy.

However, if you can survive the humiliation of metaphorically having your underwear ripped over your head, within the torn elastic band of your Fruit of the Looms lies the seed of transformation. As you grapple with your limitations, you're also forced to tap into parts of yourself you didn't know existed. You discover hidden reserves of strength, resilience, and determination. You learn to move fast, improvise, and adapt. You find new strategies to cope with and navigate the unknown. You ultimately end up with a more complete understanding of exactly what you are capable of.

By owning these moments of self-reflection, you realize it isn't just about finding order in external chaos; it's about finding order within yourself. It's about recognizing that chaos can be a powerful catalyst for growth and a pathway to becoming the most authentic and capable version of you.

Take a Moment

Regain Control

The next time you feel overwhelmed by uncertainty, pause. What one action could you take right now to regain a sense of control or calm? (Deep breath, call a friend, make a list, and so on.)

Moments to Remember:

- Uncertainty is inevitable: embrace change and adapt rather than resist it.
- Recognize when a plan isn't working and be willing to pivot.
- Uncertainty and change are inseparable travel buddies.
- Setbacks can give you the crucial information you need to overcome the obstacles you face and build the momentum you desire.
- Pivoting often requires redefining success itself.
- Chaos can be a powerful catalyst for growth and a pathway to becoming the most authentic and capable version of yourself.

4

Fix the Big Goal Glitch: Empowering True Ownership

Momentum Objectives:

- Define the Big Goal Glitch.
- Identify the root causes of the Big Goal Glitch.
- Describe the four pillars of building a culture of ownership.
- Create specific moments employees can own.

IMAGINE A LOCALLY owned company named Hometown Heating and Cooling, known for reasonable prices and personalized care. Their promise: to keep you comfortable no matter the season. The owners of this business are not just HVAC experts; they are entrepreneurs who have dreams of franchising their business one day. They enjoy serving their community and look for ways to help their customers find cost-effective solutions. They are the epitome of servant-leaders within their small community. Yet, despite their technical proficiency and commitment to customer satisfaction, something is amiss. Online reviews mention missed appointments, inconsistent service quality, and unresolved HVAC issues. Their promise of comfort is failing due to a front-line disconnect, a common challenge faced by businesses of any size. This, my friends, is the **Big Goal Glitch**: the gap between your strategic vision and frontline execution.

The Big Goal Glitch is not about having a bad plan. It is about a good plan that lacks accountability on the front lines. It's the disconnect between the well-thought-out strategy conceived by management behind closed doors and the daily realities of the employees who bring that strategy to life. It is the waiter who rushes through explanations, the factory worker cutting corners, the customer service representative who could not care less about your customers—all emblematic of a system where the front line feels disconnected from the big goals. The disconnect is often subtle but can have devastating consequences. It can breed apathy and stifle momentum. But most important, it can and does sabotage the most brilliant of plans.

What if there was a way to bridge the gap from vision to execution? What if we could turn front line workers into owners of the larger vision? What if, instead of just barking out orders, you led by giving workers the authority to make and implement decisions in how they do the work that brings the vision to life? That's what Moment Momentum is all about.

Moment Momentum isn't just an interesting idea; it is a fundamental shift in how you achieve your goals. This shift directs your approach away from a top-down mandate and instead encourages your people to create and own moments that will build momentum toward your big goals. It's about empowering every frontline worker, every cashier, every nurse, every teacher, to be accountable for their "moments" and see themselves not as someone taking orders from the ivory tower but as indispensable contributors to a shared goal.

Why is this approach so essential? When people take ownership of their work, they become much more motivated and driven. They are no longer just going through the motions but are fully engaged in the work because they believe they can affect the outcome and because they have some degree of freedom in how they do it. This shift in mindset (which we will discuss more in Chapter 7) is the key to unlocking the full potential of your workforce and transforming your organization from the inside out.

Transitioning to a Moment Momentum culture isn't always simple. It necessitates a basic change in leadership philosophy and a shift in how you approach employee empowerment. It also means confronting resistance to change, the kind that's normal in any major overhaul—especially when the overhaul is aimed at the nature and quality of a work culture. But if you want to hit those big goals, getting buy-in from those who do the work and those who manage the work is essential.

We will look more closely at the roots of the Big Goal Glitch, targeting the usual suspects that lead to a disconnect between managers and the frontline. This disconnect can take a toll on just about everything—morale, motivation, momentum, missed opportunities, and, oh yes, goals. Most important, we will lay out a practical blueprint for creating a culture of Moment Momentum with specific strategies, tools, and techniques to empower your front line and transform your organization into a well-oiled, momentum-driven machine.

The Fallout of the Big Goal Glitch

The Big Goal Glitch, that frustrating gap between a company's vision and the frontline execution of that vision, can have several causes. These causes are often self-inflicted and lead to employee disengagement and disconnection. Understanding these root causes is crucial to effectively address the problems and build a stronger, more connected organization.

The root causes of the Big Goal Glitch include the following:

- **Poor communication and lack of clarity:** When frontline workers aren't kept in the loop about the company's overall strategy, goals, and progress, they're left feeling like minions, blindly performing tasks without understanding their purpose or impact. This lack of context leads to disengagement and diminishes the sense of ownership crucial for bridging the gap of the Big Goal Glitch. Ambiguous instructions, inconsistent messaging, and a general lack of transparency further exacerbate the problem, leaving employees confused, frustrated, and, ultimately, disconnected.

- **Inadequate training and resources:** The workers on the front lines take the brunt of the difficult interactions with customers and tough operational challenges. When they are not trained properly, when they are not given the tools and access to the resources they need to do their job well, they are set up to fail. This can lead to feelings of inadequacy, resentment, and a rejection of accountability. Imagine a technician asked to install a new HVAC system without proper training on the latest technology or a hotel housekeeper expected to maintain pristine rooms without adequate cleaning supplies. The result is predictable: frustration, burnout, and a disconnect from the overall goal.

- **Meaningless work:** When employees feel that their work is unappreciated, not important, or doesn't contribute to the big goals, their motivation plummets. This is especially true for frontline workers, who often perform repetitive tasks that may seem insignificant to the big picture. Failing to connect their daily efforts to the company's overall mission creates a sense of meaningless work that has no value in achieving the big goal.

- **Bad managers:** Poor management is one of the biggest contributors to the gap between vision and execution. "Over-the-shoulder" supervision, a lack of decision-making ability, and a top-down control culture can crush creative thinking, innovation, and the willingness to own a moment—all of which are incredibly influential in creating unstoppable momentum.

The consequences of the Big Goal Glitch gap are far-reaching and potentially destructive to the entire organization. Some of these consequences include the following:

- **Decreased morale:** A "bad mood" workforce will foster negativity, cynicism, and a general feeling of "Who gives a sh*t?" This negativity can spread like the flu, poisoning the entire company culture and impacting team dynamics.
- **Productivity problems:** Disconnection to the big goal leads to missed deadlines, less productivity, and a more inefficient workforce.
- **Poor customer experience:** Disengaged employees will show a lack of motivation to go the extra mile, leading to negative reviews and pissed-off customers and sending the company's reputation into damage control.
- **Ultimate failure:** All of the negative consequences culminate in the failure to achieve the big goal, the very thing the meticulously crafted plan was designed to accomplish.

Big Goal Glitch Example: Nokia

In the early 2000s, Nokia was the undisputed king of the mobile phone market. It enjoyed a 40% market share and sold well over 100 million handsets each year. However, when Apple and Samsung entered the market with smartphone technology, Nokia's mobile phone business suffered a catastrophic disconnection between strategic vision and execution at the front line.

Nokia grappled with a major problem: it was unable to express a unified vision and strategy to its many teams. Even though the company saw that the smartphone held real promise, it could never quite get everyone on the same page, resulting in a mismatch of priorities that created internal tensions, slowed down product development, and stifled innovation.

Nokia failed to accept the necessity of features like touch screens or to see that operating systems like Android could be the future of mobile phones. This failure of belief, coupled with the belief that what they were doing was at the cutting edge, meant that they didn't invest in the necessary retraining and resources to develop technologies competitive with those of the companies that were beating them. Of course, this lack of investment also meant that their products lagged behind others in the user experience.

These disconnects had a catastrophic effect. Nokia's share of the market fell drastically, and by 2014, when it sold its mobile phone business to Microsoft, it had dropped to a paltry 3%. Nokia was once the world's largest vendor of mobile phones, but the company couldn't bridge the gap of the Big Goal Glitch.

Take a Moment

Become a Disconnection Detective

Think through your current challenges. Where is the biggest disconnection happening and why?

Building a Foundation of Ownership

Bridging the gap between strategic vision and frontline execution requires a shift in organizational culture. It begins with a conscious effort to cultivate an environment where every employee feels valued, empowered, and connected to the bigger picture. Building a culture of ownership involves four key pillars: transparent communication, comprehensive training, recognition of contributions, and employee empowerment.

Transparent Communication

Successful organizations are built on clear, consistent communication. When it comes to fostering a culture of ownership, this communication is crucial. Frontline workers need to understand not just what they're doing but why it matters. Why does that "why" matter? Explaining the rationale behind decisions, the connection between individual tasks and the overall strategy, and the impact of their work on the company's success fosters a sense of purpose and shared responsibility. This transparency builds trust, reduces uncertainty, and empowers employees to make informed decisions.

Transparent communication takes many forms:

- **Regular "Ask Me Anything" sessions with leadership:** Frontline workers have a direct line to leadership during these sessions. They can ask about the strategy and even the tactics that affect them and their work. They can also question the decisions that seem to contradict what they are being told to do or what they are being led to believe. Making them feel like their voice is heard is a powerful way to encourage accountability.
- **"Behind-the-scenes" updates and storytelling:** Providing "behind-the-scenes" looks at various departments or facets of the business helps make the front line understand the interconnectedness of the organization and its many moving parts. It brings a degree of clarity to the overall business mandate. There are multiple platforms and formats for offering this kind of insight. A short

video, for example, can easily suffice. So can the internal newsletter. Less formal structures, such as a "lunch-and-learn" session with a department, also work quite well. Showing the front line how the work is connected can inspire ownership.

- **"Reverse mentorship" program:** Reverse mentorship is pairing frontline workers with members of leadership or senior management. It presents a unique opportunity for the frontline employee to share their perspective, insight, and experience straight with leadership. It also fosters a two-way flow of information that helps dismantle the hierarchical wall. Leaders gain valuable insights into the realities of frontline work, while frontline employees gain a better understanding of the strategic challenges and priorities facing the organization.

Comprehensive Training

Providing the essential skills and knowledge to frontline workers is not just an act of individual development; it is an act of advancing the whole organization. When we invest in training, we aren't just building bridges of confidence and competence; we're enabling a sense of ownership to take root. When employees feel equipped to handle the challenges they face, they're more likely to take initiative, embrace responsibility, and provide unique contributions.

Comprehensive training goes beyond basic job skills and should include the following:

- **Scenario-based training:** Rather than merely lecturing on best practices, create realistic scenarios that simulate common customer interactions (like difficult complaints and complex requests). This allows frontline workers to practice their skills in a safe environment, enhancing their confidence to handle real-world situations once they're out of training and on their own. It helps overcome the fear of engaging and instead empowers workers to own a moment.

- **Expert-led webinars:** Engage industry experts or specialists to hold webinars and online workshops on the topics that really matter. This offers access to leading-edge knowledge and best practices that often lie outside the purview of conventional training programs. Investing in your people makes them feel like you believe in them.

- **Personalized learning plans:** Move beyond homogenized training programs and develop personalized learning plans tailored to each employee's individual needs, strengths, and career aspirations. Giving them a customized plan demonstrates your commitment to their individual growth and empowers employees to take ownership of their development.

Recognition of Contributions

Recognizing and appreciating the work of individuals—whether it is securing a huge win or completing an important task—develops a profound sense of ownership and pride among employees. When they know and feel that what they do is pivotal to the success of the organization, workers are more likely to go the extra mile, take initiative, and invest themselves fully in their work. This positive reinforcement creates a virtuous cycle, driving further engagement and strengthening ownership.

Recognition can take many forms:

- **"Story-telling campaigns":** Use both internal communication platforms and social media to tell powerful stories about the work your employees do. Share their work and their accomplishments. Highlight the ways they're impacting your organization and the customers it serves. This leads to a strong sense of ownership.

- **Perform personal thank-yous:** Something as simple as a phone call from leadership, a handwritten thank-you note, or a public acknowledgment during a team meeting can have a truly significant impact on employee morale and motivation.
- **Spontaneous recognition:** Deliver unexpected rewards that truly show your gratitude to employees making unique contributions. A personalized gift basket, a catered lunch, or a small token of appreciation delivered to their home can go a long way toward powerful recognition.

Employee Empowerment

Empowering frontline workers to make decisions within their defined roles is essential for fostering a culture of accountability. When employees feel empowered to make decisions, take initiative, and find creative solutions, they develop a stronger sense of ownership and responsibility. This autonomy allows them to truly create and own their moments.

Empowerment can be encouraged with various measures:

- **Decision-making "escape rooms":** Design escape room-style challenges that simulate real-world decision-making scenarios. These immersive experiences can help employees practice and refine their decision-making skills in a fun and engaging way and allow them to build confidence in making important decisions.
- **"Autonomy zones":** Allocate certain projects or areas of the organization to be "autonomy zones." In these designated areas, employees have full decision-making authority. This is not untethered freedom but rather a highly structured approach intended to be sandboxes for experimentation and innovation.

- **"Freedom to fail" initiatives:** Establish programs that promote intelligent risk-taking, with the understanding that not everything will pan out. Allow people to take risks, and create a safety net that ensures them they will not be penalized if some of their decisions do not work out as planned, provided that they don't make the same mistake again and learn from the failed risk.

By focusing on these four pillars—transparent communication, comprehensive training, recognition of contributions, and employee empowerment—organizations can bridge the gap and build a strong foundation of ownership. This foundation empowers frontline workers to own their moments, contribute their best work, and, ultimately, achieve the big goals that drive organizational success.

Take a Moment

Bridge the Gap

Which of the four pillars would be most impactful in bridging the gap of accountability for your current challenge? What are three specific things you could do to bridge the gap?

Implementing Moment Momentum

Frontline workers must be empowered to take ownership of the specific "moments" in their roles that are capable of creating momentum. These workers—those with the most direct and immediate interaction with customers—are in the best position to build momentum and foster a culture of accountability and continuous improvement.

Here are some concrete examples of the kinds of moments frontline employees can take ownership of:

- **Customer interactions:** Frontline employees can significantly impact customer satisfaction and loyalty. Empower them to go the extra mile by doing the following:
  - o **Providing "empowerment wallets":** Provide a budget or "empowerment wallet" to employees that allows them to do what's necessary to make customers happy, without always having to check back with a supervisor. If a customer has a complaint or issue, give employees the ability to resolve the issue and enhance the experience. This could include offering a discount, free shipping, or a complimentary service to transform a negative experience into a positive one.
- **Process improvements:** Those who work on the front lines are in the best position to spot inefficiencies and propose enhancements. Urge these employees to help in streamlining workflows and boosting efficiency by doing the following:
  - o **Introducing "bottleneck breakdowns":** Design a "bottle" that can be used when an employee identifies a bottleneck in the process. The employee will bring the bottle to a supervisor and place it on their desk, signifying that a bottleneck has been identified and an immediate solution is needed.
- **Quality control:** Quality is a shared responsibility, and frontline workers can play a pivotal role in maintaining standards by doing the following:
  - o **Granting "full-stop" privileges:** Grant employees the power to stop operations if they detect quality problems, ensuring that any defects are dealt with on the spot.

- **Problem solving:** Empower employees to identify and address challenges within their scope of work by doing the following:
  - o **Using "challenge coins":** Provide employees with "challenge coins" to use when they encounter a problem that demands immediate attention. Presenting a coin signals that the problem is serious and that the employee has a good reason for asking for time and resources to concentrate on a possible solution. This practice underscores the company's intent to deeply involve employees in problem solving and to take their insights seriously.

By building a culture of ownership among frontline workers, you are making an investment in the future. Whether that future is tomorrow, next month, or five years from now, empowering your people to own their moments means adaptability when the unexpected arises, resourcefulness in addressing new challenges, and an empowered workforce constantly seeking to innovate and improve. Building a Moment Momentum culture becomes your competitive advantage.

Moments to Remember:
- The Big Goal Glitch is the gap between your strategic vision and frontline execution.
- The root causes of the Big Goal Glitch are poor communication and clarity, inadequate training and resources, meaningless work, and bad managers.
- The four key pillars of a culture of ownership are transparent communication, comprehensive training, recognition of contributions, and employee empowerment.
- Frontline workers are in the best position to build momentum and foster a culture of accountability and continuous improvement.

5

Mitigate the Moment Thief: How Multitasking Steals Your Success

Momentum Objectives:

- Debunk the myth of multitasking.
- Learn how survival mode creates life-changing skills.
- Discover strategies for single-tasking.
- Determine how to become a "moment maker."

WE CURRENTLY LIVE in a side-hustle culture that glorifies working a 9-to-5 job, running your Amazon drop-ship company, hocking products on TikTok Shop, and successfully setting up your affiliate marketing program. This glorifying of multitasking is luring you into a dangerous world that promises more time, money, and power. All you need to do is purchase that $49 online course or sign up for the exclusive $5,000 VIP package from someone who has made all their money selling $5,000 VIP packages!

The world has become a multitasking multilevel marketing (MLM) shop, constantly vying for your most precious commodities: time and effort. If you just invest a little more time and give a little more effort, you are one step away from life-changing success. This constant striving mindset, to do and achieve more, leaves you scattered and exhausted.

You are targeted for your ambition, not knowing that the sacrifice of presence and focus will actually deter you from succeeding. You can't scroll on TikTok for more than 10 seconds without someone telling you how they made $20,000 this month using some get-rich-quick scheme that you know isn't real but you desperately want it to be.

For those of you who drank the snake oil, I have some bad news. Multitasking is a myth. It's a moment thief, robbing you of your focus and success and undermining your efforts to achieve your big goals.

The Multitasking Myth

Your brain is not wired to handle multiple complex tasks at the same time. Neuroscience has proven this over and over again. What you think is multitasking is actually your brain bouncing back and forth between individual tasks like an Olympic pickleball match. This rapid switching creates a momentary lag as your brain tries to reorient itself to a new task. The lag causes problems.

Research using driving simulators has shown that talking on a cell phone, even hands-free, impairs driving performance as much as driving under the influence. It's not because the driver is physically occupied but because the brain is rapidly switching between trying to drive and having a conversation. The lag manifests itself in delayed reaction time, missed signals, and additional risk of an accident.

Similarly, rapidly switching focus throughout the day leads to a significant drain on your mental resources. The constant shifting disrupts your momentum, increases the risk of mistakes, and jeopardizes your chance of achieving your big goal, ultimately preventing you from reaching that "flow state" where you are most productive and creative.

I can't help but think about my friends with ADHD. Due to advancements in the diagnosis and an overall better understanding of the disorder, many of my friends have received a diagnosis well into their 40s. People with ADHD aren't necessarily "choosing" to multitask; they simply have a difficult time focusing on individual tasks and filtering out distractions. The current culture plays right into the struggles those with ADHD face every day. When you factor in the constant barrage of social media, adoption of new technology, overstimulation, and an overall chaotic world, it's a relentless daily battle. All of that is to say that if you've been diagnosed with ADHD, these strategies will be even more difficult to employ. But with practice, persistence, and proper medication, you can do this.

The Hidden Cost of Rapid Task-Switching

The many hidden costs of multitasking extend well beyond disrupting momentum and making mistakes. The latest research has shown that chronic multitasking can lead to the following:

- **Weakened cognitive control:** Your ability to maintain focus and filter out distractions is reduced, making you more susceptible to potential interruptions and impulsive decisions.
- **Impaired memory and learning:** When your brain is playing pickleball, it struggles to decipher information effectively, making it more difficult to learn and retain new knowledge.
- **Less creativity and problem-solving ability:** Being able to get into a deep state of flow is when we are most creative and can innovate. Multitasking stops the flow.

- **More stress and anxiety:** The constant switching adds pressure and leads to chronic stress that impacts your mental and physical health.
- **Missed moments:** When you are constantly distracted with multiple tasks, you are less present and miss opportunities that are right in front of you.

In a world that worships looking busy and being constantly connected, the allure of multitasking can be incredibly strong. However, the science is clear: multitasking comes at a significant cost. If you can recognize the true toll of dividing your attention, you can pivot, regain your focus, and reclaim the present moment.

I witnessed the real danger of multitasking during one of my son's many hospitalizations. On one particular admittance, Theo was being treated for extremely high potassium, a common struggle for patients on dialysis. Most of these admittances happen through the emergency room. The emergency room is a chaotic place where doctors, nurses, patients, and family members are trying to stay out of each other's way while simultaneously trying to get each other's attention. It is a multitasking mecca.

During the admitting process, the doctor on call had mistakenly ordered a bag of potassium to be given to Theo. The hospital pharmacy didn't notice the error, and the nurse on duty didn't check his chart. Before we knew it, the potassium bag was hung, and the nurse was getting ready to connect it to his IV. We noticed the error and asked the nurse what she was doing. Administering a bag of potassium to a patient being treated for high potassium is a death sentence. Having lived in a hospital for almost a year, I understand the amount of multitasking that happens when you are understaffed and overworked. But when you are in an industry where life and death are on the line, multitasking can become a dangerous game.

What are the stakes at your job if splitting your focus over multiple tasks at the same time is hurting your ability to process vital information? What are the consequences of that vital information not being shared with appropriate stakeholders? The potential for catastrophic consequences grows with each task not getting your full attention. There is a better way to approach your work and life.

Take a Moment

The True Toll

How many of the hidden costs of multitasking have you experienced? Which one is creating the biggest challenge for you currently?

Reclaiming Your Moments: Strategies for Single-Tasking

The incessant chasing after the idea of "doing it all"—the seductive call of multitasking—often leaves you feeling unfocused and unproductive. Rather than making progress on a handful of goals at the same time, your scattered energy better serves you when it is funneled into a single task, allowing the brain to operate in "task exclusive" mode. By dedicating your full attention to one task at a time, you achieve a deeper level of concentration, fostering the ability to create Moment Momentum. This focused approach not only leads to higher quality work but also generates a sense of accomplishment as you complete each task, building momentum toward larger goals.

If you are feeling a little disheartened that you spend a lot of time multitasking, it's okay. You can retrain your brain to focus and resign your position in the multitasking MLM. Here are some practical strategies to mitigate the moment thief and reclaim your momentum:

- **Plan your priorities:** Decide which tasks are most crucial and schedule dedicated time to address them in order of importance. You can use time-blocking strategies to create focused work blocks. Set a timer on your phone for a specific time and avoid distractions. Be deliberate with your intention.
- **Control your environment:** Pick a quiet place where you can focus. Turn off notifications on your phone and laptop. The environment can help you get into a flow state much faster if you are cognizant of your surroundings.
- **Build in breaks:** The very idea of working on a task for an extended period of time can be enough to distract you. Build in breaks to be able to maintain your focus and concentration and prevent burning out. Step away from the task every 20 minutes or so for a short breather. Take a quick walk, do some stretching, or step outside to get some fresh air.
- **Identify the "one thing":** Identify the single most important task you must complete before the end of the day. Focus your attention on completing this task at all costs. This way, at the end of the day, you can at least know you have accomplished the "one thing" you needed to.
- **Match up your tasks:** Try to group similar tasks together to minimize switching. For example, respond to all emails at once rather than breaking them up throughout the day. This will allow your brain to focus and get into a rhythm while reducing mental fatigue.
- **Use technology:** Utilize productivity tools that you have available to help you stay on track. Phone timers, notification blockers, and door signs can be incredibly useful.

- **Celebrate and show yourself kindness:** Learning to break your multitasking habits will take time, effort, and patience. Learn to celebrate when you successfully focus on a single task and show some self-compassion when you fail.

In the wise words of GI Joe, "Now you know. And knowing is half the battle." But knowing alone isn't going to change anything. You have to be willing to try these strategies. See which ones work for you and which don't—one at a time. So pick one and see what happens.

Take a Moment

Selecting a Single-Tasking Strategy

Choose and then analyze which of the mitigating-the-moment-thief strategies described in this chapter will be most effective in addressing the hidden costs of multitasking that you identified in the previous exercise, "The True Toll."

Becoming Moment Makers

By understanding the science behind why multitasking doesn't work and implementing some practical strategies, you can reclaim the power of individual moments. Being fully present allows you to gather a wealth of information that often goes unnoticed in the whirlwind of multitasking. You become more in tune with your thoughts, feelings, and intuitions. Your heightened awareness allows you to have a deeper understanding of the context you are operating within, enabling you to make better decisions.

With this new strategy, you can act with deliberate intention. Your actions are no longer reactive, driven by the urgency of the latest notification or demand, but proactive, guided by a new-found clarity. You are now refocusing your energy and resources on the tasks that truly matter, maximizing your impact and building the momentum that will lead you to your goals.

This shift from scattered attention to a more focused presence will transform how you approach challenges. Instead of feeling overwhelmed, you can direct your full mental process toward potential solutions.

Your journey to becoming a moment maker is not about adding more hours to the day. It's about maximizing the impact of each moment. It's shifting from the idea of constant busyness to intentional focus, recognizing that real productivity lies not in doing more but in doing what matters most.

This sort of thing doesn't happen overnight. It requires letting go of the idea of multitasking and all it represents. But I promise the rewards will be worth the effort. You will find yourself less stressed, less anxious, and more deeply connected to everything around you. By reclaiming your time and effort, you can refocus it on creating momentum for yourself and for those you love.

Moments to Remember:
- Multitasking is a moment thief that steals your focus and hinders your success.
- Single-tasking is a strategy that will help you regain your momentum.
- Focusing on a single moment allows you to become more in tune with your thoughts, feelings, and intuitions.
- Real productivity lies not in doing more but in doing what matters most.

PART

II

The Blueprint

6

Understand the Three Stages of Momentum: Learning to Recognize Where You Are

Momentum Objectives:

- Understand the three stages of momentum.
- Identify which stage of momentum you are in.
- Recognize the interplay between the stages of momentum.
- Acknowledge the cyclical nature of momentum.

THE CONCEPT OF momentum, specifically in the context of personal and professional development, isn't a linear progression but rather a dynamic interplay of three different stages: *Living*, *Lifting*, and *Legacy*. Each stage is distinct in its focus and characteristics. They are not fixed destinations but, instead, fluid stages that you may cycle through multiple times over the course of your life.

Understanding the stages of momentum and recognizing where you currently stand allows you to tailor your strategy and approach your goals with more clarity and intention. Grasping these stages also provides a crucial framework for understanding where others are so you can offer empathy and support based on their specific stage.

These three stages are interconnected and often influence each other. Sometimes you may find yourself straddling two different stages at the same time or even experiencing a temporary regression to a previous stage based on what life looks like at the moment. The complexity of life in real time forces you to dance around setbacks, embrace the small wins, harness any progress you can, and learn to continuously adapt to your circumstances. By understanding the three stages of momentum, you can better navigate the challenges and focus your intention and attention on moving forward toward your big goals.

Stage 1: Living—The Foundation of Momentum

The first stage of momentum, Living, isn't about thriving; it's about surviving. It's the foundation upon which all other momentum is built. Here, the focus is the immediate moment. Long-term goals fade into the distance as urgent needs grab all your attention. This isn't necessarily a negative thing; it's a reality for many, especially those just starting out or facing unexpected challenges.

As a child of the 70s and 80s, it's hard to understand the real-life challenges that face young adults today. When you grow up drinking from a garden hose, playing with sticks, and impatiently waiting for your favorite song to be played on the radio, it's hard to find empathy for a generation that "has had it easy." But the truth is the world has changed. Try paying a couple hundred bucks for rent, 99 cents for gas, $2 to go to a movie, or buying a car for under $30K these days. Oh, and the wages have not grown in tandem with the cost of living. Gen Z's struggles are very real. They are simply different than ours were.

We have a dear friend of our daughter, Alex, who is a 24-year-old recent college graduate. She lives in a hip, live-work-play, master-planned community among her peers who all face similar circumstances. Like many of her peers, Alex is navigating the realities of adulthood in a world that feels increasingly unstable. Despite that shiny master's degree from an impressive university, Alex can't afford to work in the field she wants to, so she takes a job as a flight attendant. The crazy schedule, uncertain hours, and moderate paycheck force her into the survival mode that many Gen Zers are facing right now.

Alex's primary concern is finances. The big rent number, car payment, insurance, cell phone, and student loans looming over her make it hard to eat well, work out, or take care of herself. The financial pressure keeps Alex in a hyper state of anxiety as she can focus only on how many trips she will need to fly to cover her expenses and whether she has enough money to buy groceries this week before she gets paid. She manages to do all of this while feeling depressed that she isn't pursuing the job she truly wants and isn't moving her life forward in any significant way. Her dreams and aspirations have been temporarily shelved as they are simply inaccessible in the face of immediate survival.

This survival mode is an all-too-common experience for many in today's economic climate. The rising cost of living, limp wages, and dicey employment options create a perfect storm for this type of existence. It can be incredibly difficult to break this cycle as the demands of the present consume all your available energy and resources.

For Alex and countless others like her, "living" becomes synonymous with just getting by, working paycheck to paycheck, hoping desperately for the break that will move them forward toward their goals. While it can be difficult to see when you are living in survival mode, this stage, while challenging, isn't without its benefits. Working through survival mode can teach you life-changing skills such as the following:

- **Building resilience:** When individuals must live in survival mode, they often adapt swiftly and well to their ever-changing and challenging circumstances, developing resilience in the face of adversity.
- **Developing resourcefulness:** When resources are scant, individuals in survival mode often find creative ways to solve problems and use what they have to the fullest. This invaluable skill serves them well in both their personal and professional lives.
- **Learning to prioritize:** Survival mode is a potent teacher of prioritization skills. When life's demands winnow down to their essentials, you often are forced to get better at making decisions that will stick. When you emerge from survival mode, you usually retain some of the skills acquired: time management, stronger decisions, and more critical thinking.
- **Cultivating greater empathy and compassion:** When we go through hard times, our understanding and kindness toward others who are also experiencing tough times increase. This dynamic can build an atmosphere of love and support in our relationships and communities.
- **Improving mental toughness:** Always being in survival mode can be tough on your brain. Yet facing constant challenges can pave the way to a more robust mental toughness and a mindset that is better at enduring hard times.
- **Building confidence:** When people maneuver through tough situations, they build confidence that they have what it takes to deal with difficult obstacles and navigate uncertainty.

Taking these powerful lessons and newfound skills out of the hardship of survival mode can become the catalyst for powerful transformation that leads to the second stage of momentum: Lifting.

Stage 2: Lifting—A Shift in Desire and Expectation

The second stage, Lifting, marks an important turning point in the momentum journey. There comes a point when you get tired of surviving and will stop at nothing to move closer to your goals. You experience a shift in desire and expectation. Desire serves as the spark, and expectation becomes the fuel. Together, these two forces create hope. The more we desire something and the clearer our expectations are, the more hope we have.

During the 1950s, Curt Richter, a scientist at Johns Hopkins University, conducted what turned out to be a profound experiment on "hope." He placed rats into buckets of water and timed how long they could swim before they gave up. It turns out that rats are strong swimmers; they lasted an average of 15 minutes before they began to drown. With the baseline established, Richter placed a rat in a bucket of water, and just as the time reached 15 minutes, before the rat gave up, he reached in and pulled the rat out of the water. He dried the rat off, gave it a second to catch its breath, and then immediately placed the rat back into the bucket of water to see how long it would swim the second time. He conducted this experiment on many rats. How long do you think these rats swam after they were placed back in the bucket of water? Another 15 minutes? 30 minutes? Would you believe me if I told you the rats swam for nearly 60 hours?! This study revealed something incredible about hope.

If you believe your circumstances are temporary and change is possible, you become capable of extraordinary things.

This is the core message of the Lifting stage: the realization that your limitations are often self-imposed and that hope can shatter those perceived boundaries. When you enter the Lifting stage, you begin to do the following:

- **Recognize and confront your excuses:** Breaking free from survival mode forces you to confront your excuses head-on. It's painful but also quite enlightening because when you're faced with the essential question of "Why am I not doing this?" you either have to come up with a pretty weak excuse or else admit that you're just not that motivated. Facing this truth can clear away your fog of excuses and lead to a strong, newfound sense of empowerment.
- **Take ownership of your circumstances:** When uncertainty is constantly challenging you, you learn to take responsibility for your decisions and actions and don't allow your circumstances to dictate what's possible. You decide to take control and act with deliberate intention.
- **Start supportive self-talk:** When lifting yourself to the next level of momentum, you are more careful with the inner dialogue going on as you need to surround yourself with support. That support starts within and plays a major role in your ability to create momentum.
- **Shift from "Why me?" to "What if?":** Moving from a victim mentality to a mindset of possibilities creates a new path for creativity and problem-solving to travel. When you're faced with a problem and you ask yourself "What if" instead of "Why me?" you're consciously setting the problem up as something that can be overcome and that can yield a potentially better solution than the one you have at the moment.

The Lifting stage is all about exploration and growth. It's where you step beyond the old boundaries to see how far you can push them. It's the climb from the bottom rung of the "getting by" ladder to the overlooking heights of purpose and fulfillment. It's the moment you decide to lift yourself toward your full potential. The rise to the top unlocks something within you that fuels the need to share what you've learned.

> ## Take a Moment
>
> ## How High Can You Go?
>
> What are the self-imposed limitations you have placed on yourself? How will you generate enough hope to shatter those limitations?

Stage 3: Legacy—Creating Momentum for Others

Once you've achieved a certain level of success, you progress to the Legacy stage of momentum. This stage is not solely defined by how financially successful you have been or how many goals you have crushed. It represents a shift in perspective from personal growth to a desire to uplift those around you. It's the realization that the impact you leave behind is as important as any personal success you have achieved. I truly believe that this is how people will remember you. This is the very essence of legacy… generating momentum for others.

Taylor Swift is a perfect example of someone living the Legacy stage, as she is known for her ability and desire to create momentum for up-and-coming artists. She has done this throughout her career. She shined a light on Ed Sheeran in 2013, as he opened for her on her Red Tour. They even collaborated on the song "Everything Has Changed," which they performed together on tour. Sheeran has gone on to sell out arenas and win four Grammy Awards. They have continued to collaborate with their latest song, "End Game," which also features the artist Future. Taylor did it again by elevating Shawn Mendez on her 1989 World Tour, by giving him an opening slot and exposing him to her massive fanbase, and with Camila Cabello on the Reputation Tour. In fact, on her latest album, *The Tortured Poets Department*, she merely mentioned Charlie Puth's name on the title track, saying that he "should be a bigger artist," and Puth saw a huge uptick in social media interest. The increased attention provided Charlie with a platform to release new music and amplified interest in his previously recorded work.

The Legacy stage is often accompanied by a profound sense of gratitude. You have weathered the Living stage and learned the hard lessons. You have pulled yourself up through the Lifting stage and now recognize that you didn't accomplish any of this solely on your own. You begin to take note of the support and opportunities that propelled you along the way. The gratitude now has you wanting to pay it forward. You now understand that success is a collaborative effort.

The Legacy stage can manifest itself in a variety of ways:

- **Mentoring:** People in the Legacy stage usually feel a deep sense of fulfillment from the act of passing on their wisdom and experiences. When you mentor a colleague or a budding entrepreneur, you're doing much more than "helping the next generation." You're offering up some of the knowledge that you've acquired (often the hard way) to serve as a guidepost for them. And in my experience, that's always a two-way street. You reinforce your own learning by "going through the motions" of mentorship while simultaneously serving as an agent of growth and development for someone else creating momentum for both of you.

- **Advocating:** The Legacy stage often comes with a deep sense of gratitude for what you've have accomplished. You understand that success is a team effort and often feel compelled to put your voice and influence to work for social justice causes. This commitment can help drive momentum and meaningful change in society, addressing inequalities and making a difference in the lives of those who are marginalized or disadvantaged.

- **Volunteering:** Recognizing the support and opportunities that have contributed to your success, volunteering becomes a powerful way to pay it forward. By identifying and volunteering for organizations whose work you would like to contribute to, you can provide essential support, create momentum, and help improve the quality of life for others, fostering a sense of community and collective responsibility.

- **Creating:** Inspiring and uplifting people through artistic means—be it writing, painting, music, or some other artistic pursuit—can be a powerful way of creating momentum for others while establishing a strong legacy. This form of legacy not only enriches the cultural landscape but also serves as a testament to the power of creativity and expression in connecting with and motivating others.

The common thread is that you are focused on empowering others to achieve their full potential and create their own momentum. There is no seeking accolades or recognition here. It's about real service and pure intention. You are looking for impact more than anything else, fostering a sense of connection and purpose.

You've probably never heard of the Australian with a golden arm, James Harrison. Harrison donated blood nearly every week for more than 60 years. His blood contained a rare antibody that is used to create a treatment for Rhesus disease, a potentially fatal condition for unborn babies. Over the course of his life, Harrison's donations are credited with saving more than 2 million infants. His selfless act has created a legacy that will last well beyond his lifetime and continues to inspire others to step up and donate whenever possible. Something as simple as donating blood has literally given life to an entirely new generation.

Take a Moment

A Short Note

Name someone who has generated momentum for you. Write a short note or compose a quick email thanking them for their investment in you and explaining how it has affected you.

The Dynamic Interplay Between Stages

The interplay between the three stages is dynamic and often cyclical. The resilience built in the Living stage becomes the foundation for the ambition and determination of the Lifting stage. The growth and experiences of the Lifting stage inform the new perspective and motivation for the Legacy stage. Having experienced all the struggle and success, those in the Legacy stage possess a unique understanding of the entire journey and a true appreciation for the support received along the way.

The interconnectedness of these stages is key to understanding the cyclical nature of momentum. Sometimes, sh*t hits the fan and spins your life upside down, causing a temporary regression to Living, even if you were comfortably in the Legacy stage. These stages are not fixed destinations. They are fluid; you will move between them throughout your entire life.

The COVID-19 pandemic showed just how fragile momentum can be and how the three stages can interact at a moment's notice.

Sarah began her culinary career by washing dishes and prepping ingredients in a busy local restaurant. The long hours, low pay, and relentless conditions were her Living reality. She was in full survival mode, just trying to cover rent and make ends meet. She learned to be resilient, cut expenses, and live as lean as possible. After months of sucking it up, she became tired of merely surviving and dreamed of opening her own restaurant one day. She enrolled in culinary school at night, working double shifts to pay for her dream. Her work ethic Lifted her to another level of success. She excelled in her classes, was recognized for her talent, and ended up landing a job as a sous chef at a fine dining restaurant in town. Fast-forward a few years, and Sarah became the owner of a very successful contemporary restaurant. Her financial success allowed her to take risks with hiring young aspiring chefs and sending them to culinary classes at the local college. Just as Sarah began to see her restaurant skyrocket, COVID-19 hit, bleeding her dry of every ounce of her savings and forcing her to close the doors on her dream. This is the cyclical nature of momentum. Despite the enormous setback, Sarah did not give up. She started a small catering business out of her house, adapting to the uncertainty of the moment. Sarah's story isn't over; it's simply starting a new chapter. All of the skills and perseverance she learned years ago are about to become the difference in her reemerging to find success once again.

Ultimately, the three stages of momentum are about self-discovery, personal growth, and unique contribution. As you learn to navigate each of them, you will gain a deeper appreciation for just how fragile the world can be and what your place is within it, just as Sarah did. The ups and downs are to be expected, as is your positive mindset along the journey, which we will tackle next.

Moments to Remember:

- The three stages of momentum are not fixed destinations but, instead, are fluid stages that you may cycle through multiple times throughout your life.
- The Living stage embraces "survival mode" as a way to build the crucial skills necessary to lift yourself out of your current circumstances.
- The Lifting stage amplifies your desires and expectations to motivate you to reach another level of success.
- The amount of hope you have is directly proportionate to your desires and expectations.
- If you believe that your circumstances are temporary and change is possible, you are capable of extraordinary things.
- The Legacy stage is all about creating momentum for others.
- The interconnectedness of these stages is key to understanding the cyclical nature of momentum.

7

Adopt the WITWAW Mindset: Turning Probabilities into Possibilities

Momentum Objectives:

- Understand the "what if there was a way" (WITWAW) mindset and how it can transform probabilities into possibilities.
- Learn how to shift from reacting to moments to becoming an architect of them.
- Explore the concept of turning obstacles into opportunities.
- Discover how adopting a WITWAW mindset is transforming different industries.

IN THE HEART of Ypsilanti, Michigan, the Eastern Michigan University Eagles prepared for another season. Zack Conti, a walk-on offensive lineman, had become a quiet force over the previous four years. He worked tirelessly, earning his spot as the projected starter at left tackle for the 2023 season. He wasn't a showboat, nor did he seek attention; he just put his head down and did the work necessary to get things done. His commitment to his team and the game he loved was admirable. But that commitment came at a price, as Zack was not on scholarship and had to work multiple jobs to pay for school and make ends meet. He worked a landscaping job and tore out tile and carpet for his father's company on the side. The financial strain was feeling insurmountable, and he began to think about entering the transfer portal to see if a smaller school might offer him a scholarship to play. Conti's teammate, two-time captain and fellow offensive lineman Brian Dooley, knew that Zack worked hard to cover his costs to play football, but when he heard that Zack was selling his plasma just to be able to suit up for the season, he knew something had to be done.

Rather than just accepting the probable fact that there were no additional scholarships to be awarded, Brian shifted his thoughts to finding possibilities to help. He approached his head coach, Chris Creighton, with a wild idea: to gift his scholarship to Zack. The coach was stunned, as never in his years of coaching had such a selfless act been volunteered. Brian had already spoken with his parents about what he wanted to do. They would find a way to cover the $25,000 they needed to empower their son to change his teammate's life.

During a preseason team meeting, Coach Creighton explained his frustration of not having enough scholarships for the players who deserved them. He then explained what Brian Dooley was proposing to do and asked Brian to stand. Brian walked over to Zack and handed him the official papers to acknowledge Zack being placed on scholarship. The team erupted in a wild celebration.

Brian Dooley's intentional sacrifice went on to earn him the 2023 Disney Spirit Award as the most inspirational player in college football.

Finding the Possibilities

Transformational moments rarely happen by accident. You don't just stumble upon them. They are cultivated, crafted, and coaxed into being—by you or someone else. This chapter is about rewiring your mindset to change what's possible. It's about shifting from reacting to moments to becoming an architect of them, just as Brian Dooley did. He didn't accept the probable lack of scholarships. He looked for possibilities. That is what I call a *WITWAW* mindset.

Your mind is hardwired to protect itself, quick to erect impenetrable walls to shield you from potential discomfort or failure. But these walls are often rooted in fear and limit your ability to see beyond them. If you want to create the conditions to capture a transformational moment, you can't be the helpless princess in the tower waiting to be saved. You need to embrace a different approach. It's time to pull up your hair, Rapunzel.

The WITWAW mindset turns probabilities into possibilities. It's about shifting your internal dialogue: obstacles become opportunities, challenges become invitations to learn and grow, and setbacks become stepping stones.

Creating transformational moments is not only about grand gestures or life-altering events. It's about approaching everyday interactions with intentionality, curiosity, and a willingness to be present. It's about shifting from reacting to crafting and from transactional exchanges to meaningful connections. It's about believing that even the smallest moments, when infused with the right elements, have the power to create a ripple effect, transforming not just your own life, but the lives of those around you.

In the twenty-first century, the adoption of a WITWAW mindset is enabling companies to experience significant breakthroughs across industries:

- **Healthcare:** Artificial intelligence (AI) is being used to diagnose diseases more quickly and accurately. AI algorithms are now capable of analyzing medical images, predicting patient outcomes, and even personalizing treatment plans. Someone had to ask, "What if there was a way to use AI to improve patient treatment?"

- **Farming:** The use of vertical farming, where crops are grown in stacked layers within controlled environments, is allowing the growth of crops in urban areas. Again, someone had to ask, "What if there was a way to grow food in the city?"
- **Aerospace:** SpaceX has developed reusable rockets that have considerably lowered the cost of space exploration and led to innovations in commercial space travel. The question of "What if there was a way to reuse the launch rockets?" had to be asked.

All of these improvements have been made possible by asking "What if there was a way?" in the face of accepted probability. The WITWAW mindset is just as effective much closer to home. Try asking yourself, what if there was a way to spend more time with my family? To overcome my fear of public speaking? To make better choices with my food? To lose the weight that is making me unhealthy? To strengthen my marriage? Using the WITWAW mindset can and will lead to improvements throughout your entire life.

WITWAW in Action

To implement the framework of the WITWAW mindset, follow these six steps:

1. **Identify the challenge:** This step consists of identifying the challenges or constraints that you are currently facing in a certain situation. It requires a genuine evaluation of the present condition and the problems that need to be addressed.
2. **Ask the WITWAW question:** This important step is all about pushing against the status quo and asking

"What if there was a way?" This question prompts us to tap into our sources of curiosity and to explore options well outside of the normal way of doing things.

3. **Explore possibilities:** Once you ask the WITWAW question, you can start to actively pursue and think through new ideas and approaches, being as open as possible to the kinds of things that might happen if you choose to go in one direction rather than another. You seek and consider the possibilities that exist beyond the current confines of your work—beyond its existing limitations.

4. **Turn probabilities into possibilities:** This step is about taking the potential opportunity you have and figuring out exactly what you can do with it. You must assess the feasibility and desirability of potential new ideas and move from theoretical opportunities to practical solutions.

5. **Realize the possibility:** The implementation of the possibilities explored occurs at this step. This is where the new solution moves to market, ensuring that it reaches the people who can benefit from it the most. And don't forget: "actualizing the possibility" isn't just for startups and corporate innovation. You can be the "possibility evangelist" inside your organization too.

6. **Create transformational impact:** The last step centers on the wider implications of the new solution. It concerns seeing the innovative approach as it really is, not as a temporary fix but as a true disruption in the way things are done, which can change the way many individuals (and potentially entire organizations) achieve outcomes.

If we look at the recent meteoric rise of the GLP-1 weight-loss drugs as a case study, we can see how they might have implemented the framework of the WITWAW mindset:

1. **Identify the challenge:** Semaglutide was first developed as a treatment for Type 2 diabetes to help control blood

sugar levels in the body. However, when it underwent clinical testing, investigators found that not only was it effective at regulating blood sugar levels, it was causing something of a side effect—weight loss—for many who were taking it.

2. **Ask the WITWAW question:** Researchers and pharmaceutical companies embraced the WITWAW mindset by asking "What if there was a way to harness this side effect to create an effective weight loss treatment?"

3. **Explore possibilities:** Rather than considering weight loss as just a side effect of semaglutide, scientists looked more deeply into its potential uses. They conducted further research studies to see if semaglutide could be safe and effective enough to be used as a drug for significant weight loss.

4. **Turn probabilities into possibilities:** By shifting their focus from the drug's original purpose, researchers transformed the probability of a side effect into the possibility of a new, effective treatment for obesity. This approach involved rigorous testing and validation to ensure the drug's safety and efficacy for weight management.

5. **Realize the possibility:** The end result was the creation and authorization of drugs such as Wegovy®, which are intended to manage weight and have been effective for many patients dealing with obesity.

6. **Create transformational impact:** This discovery not only provided a new tool for weight management but also demonstrated the power of curiosity and the WITWAW mindset in driving innovation. It highlighted how questioning assumptions and exploring new possibilities can lead to groundbreaking advancements in healthcare.

> **Take a Moment**
>
> **Perceiving Possibilities**
>
> What are three current challenges in your life that would benefit from a WITWAW mindset? How would your life look different if you were successful in finding a way to navigate these challenges?

Embracing Curiosity

Curiosity may have killed the cat, but it is the engine that drives the WITWAW mindset. It's how you become actively engaged with the world around you. Here are some practical ways you can become a more curious person:

- **Question everything:** Even though it may feel like you are being a pain when you ask questions, you need to learn to question everything. This is how you gain valuable insights. If you ask with genuine curiosity and not as an interrogation, you will find people are much more amenable to answering your questions. Something as simple as "This seems to be something that you genuinely care about, Frank. I'm curious, is there a reason why?"
- **Cultivate a first-time focus:** Learn to approach situations as if it were the first time you encountered them. Try not to bring your preconceived notions or assumptions to the table. This allows you to see things with "fresh" eyes and an open heart. Instead of going into your next meeting with a "not this again" approach, try to learn something new about your colleagues or the project. Even if you've done a particular task the same way 100 different times, look for an improved way to get the job done.

- **Challenge your biases:** Engage with people from all walks of life. Grow your knowledge of other cultures, backgrounds, and viewpoints. Watch some documentaries, read some books, ask someone to dinner, and expand your horizons.
- **Fight your boredom:** Rather than mindlessly scrolling through social media, use your time to explore something new. Boredom is often a sign of untapped curiosity. Pick a specific subject you are interested in and dig deeper. Learn more about that river cruise in Portugal, the statue in the park down the road, or that dog breed you have been thinking about adopting. No matter what, be intentional with your time.
- **Be a better listener:** Listen to learn, not to respond. Ask some clarifying questions like "Can you elaborate on that for me?" or "What led you to that conclusion?" Take a genuine interest in what's being said. This will lead to more meaningful connections.
- **Keep a curiosity list:** Keep a list dedicated to things you want to learn more about. Instead of just thinking "That's interesting," add your curiosity to the list. "How much do hummingbirds eat?" "How long do butterflies live?" "How many licks does it take to get to the center of a Tootsie Roll pop?" (The answer is 3 ... again, I got you Gen Z.)
- **Set a curious clock:** We often get so busy that we don't leave time to be curious. Set a short timer for dedicated curiosity. Even 10 minutes can expand your viewpoint and make you a more well-rounded human.

Take a Moment

Start Your Curiosity List

Create your first entry on your Curiosity List. What are three things you have always been curious about but never looked deeper into? Devote 10 minutes a day to discovering something new about them.

Curiosity Pioneers

Some of the most impressive accomplishments in human history have occurred because of a driving curiosity. This essential human trait pushes us to evolve, discover, and innovate. Think about some of the most impressive humans in history:

- **Leonardo da Vinci:** He was obsessed with art, science, engineering, and human anatomy as well as countless other fields. He wasn't content with mastering just one of these areas; he wanted to master *all* of them. Without his insatiable curiosity, we wouldn't have the *Mona Lisa*, helicopters, tanks, machine guns, diving suits, parachutes, hang gliders, or dozens of other creations.
- **Marie Curie:** Her devout interest in radioactivity led to the discovery of two new elements, polonium and radium. This set the stage for advancements in cancer treatment and the development of portable X-ray machines, eventually saving millions of lives.
- **Albert Einstein:** His curiosity about the nature of space, time, and gravity led to the theory of relativity, arguably the most significant scientific breakthrough of the twentieth century. He is credited with numerous other discoveries and contributions to theoretical physics. His relentless asking of "Why?" literally transformed our understanding of the universe.

Now listen, you may be saying to yourself, "I'm no Einstein," but the truth is the real genius of curiosity lies in its potential to ignite discovery and innovation in all of us. Maybe you figure out how to carry the car seat and groceries while holding your other child's hand. Maybe you concoct a cleaning paste of baking soda, vinegar, and orange peels that removes that stubborn stain on the glass cooktop. Maybe you figure out exactly how to handle that narcissist at work or maybe you discover that one of your great-grandfathers was an actual saint (that's right ... I'm part saint ... I won't ask you to kiss my ring ... a simple kneeling will suffice).

You don't need to be a genius to change the world. You can start by just changing your perspective, adopting a WITWAW mindset, and unlocking your true potential. You simply need to be curious, accept the possibilities that arise, and reject the probability of failure—no matter what your inner dialogue is trying to convince you of.

Moments to Remember:

- Transformational moments rarely happen by accident; they are cultivated, crafted, and coaxed into being—by you or someone else.
- Your mind is hardwired to protect itself, quick to erect impenetrable walls to shield you from potential discomfort or failure.
- The WITWAW mindset turns probabilities into possibilities.
- Creating transformational moments is not only about grand gestures or life-altering events. It's about approaching everyday interactions with intentionality, curiosity, and a willingness to be present.
- Curiosity is the engine that drives the WITWAW mindset.
- The real genius of curiosity lies in its potential to ignite discovery and innovation in all of us.

8

Crush the Critic: Outmaneuvering Your Inner Nemesis

Momentum Objectives:

- Identify and understand your inner critic.
- Recognize the common tactics of your inner critic.
- Discover strategies for managing your inner critic.
- Learn to reframe negative thoughts.
- Build a balanced support system.
- Foster self-compassion.

LET'S TALK ABOUT that annoying, petulant voice that lives inside your head and loves to question everything. In the previous chapter, we talked about being genuinely curious, but here we will be talking about casting doubt. The casting doubt voice likes to second-guess your every move and turn a potential flaw into a full-blown Broadway production. This is your *inner critic*, the relentless nemesis that's out to crush your dreams, stop your momentum, and make you afraid of your own shadow.

You know the routine. Your inner critic may start out seemingly concerned: "Are you sure you have the skills to accomplish this goal? I mean, I applaud the ambition, but do you really want to look like a fool if things don't pan out?" This conniving master puppeteer will feign empathy and concern, while secretly plotting to knock you on your ass and extract every ounce of hope it can from you.

It may sound and sometimes feel like there is a demon living inside you, but the truth is your inner critic isn't a human flaw; it's part of the human condition. It's been an integral part of human evolution for millennia. It was designed to keep you safe and thus is engrained in how you approach uncertain situations. It is there to stop you from taking perceived risks, which, unfortunately, will prevent you from experiencing real growth and fulfillment.

What if there was a way to turn your inner critic into an unexpected ally? (See what I did there?) Let's dive a little deeper into the origins of your inner tormentor, unmask its hidden agenda, and learn how to redirect its power.

Origins of the Inner Critic

Where does your critic come from, and how did it get here? It comes from a cauldron of evolutionary instinct, social expectations, and personal experiences. Back when your great, great, great, great ... you get it ... grandfather was dodging saber-toothed tigers, a little self-doubt kept him from being dinner for Tony the Tiger. Fast-forward 14,000 years, and that same instinct doesn't know when to quit. It has a hard time understanding that all risks aren't the same, so it simply tries to block anything when facing uncertainty.

The inner critic is a master of disguise, adept at using various tactics to slow down your progress. Its ultimate goal is to stop you from gaining momentum by convincing you of its false narratives.

The inner critic's ability to shape-shift allows it to manifest itself in a variety of ways:

- **Perfectionism:** Perfectionism often represents the inner critic's most direct—not to mention damaging—incarnation. Its voice demands unrealistically high standards. It tells you that anything less than perfect is indeed worthless, leading to endless tweaking and revisions or even abandoning projects altogether. This mindset can prevent you from seeing any progress and learning from your mistakes, ultimately stalling your growth and crushing momentum.
- **Procrastination:** By morphing into procrastination, the inner critic leads you to believe you are delaying action because you are not yet ready to take that action. It tricks you into believing that conditions must be ideal before you start, causing missed opportunities and compounding stress. Yet holding off like this usually just accumulates extra stress and missed opportunities. After a while, you start to trust yourself less, and your confidence dwindles.
- **Fear of failure:** The inner critic uses the fear of failure as a potent tool to keep you in line, trying to paralyze you with anxiety about not succeeding. It tries to get you to think about every potential negative outcome, leading you to not take risks and to avoid new challenges. This fear can prevent you from realizing your potential, stifle creativity and innovation, and stop momentum.
- **Sabotage:** The inner critic sabotages you by telling you convincing lies that feel like the undeniable truth. It uses self-doubt and negative self-talk to undermine your confidence, making it difficult to challenge the false narratives. Recognizing and confronting these lies is crucial to overcome the critic's influence.

The first step in outmaneuvering your inner critic is recognizing its patterns. While it may be shifty in its approach, it often uses the same old tactics. It may be helpful to write down the things your critic says to you repeatedly and keep them filed in an *Inner Critic Inventory* that you can reference when your inner critic voice gets louder than you'd like. The sooner you recognize it, the less power it will have over you.

Take a Moment

Catch the Critic

For one day, carry a small notebook or use your phone to jot down every time you recognize your inner critic raising its voice. Write down exactly what it says. These writings will become the beginning of your Inner Critic Inventory.

Challenging the Validity of What Your Inner Critic Tells You

Once you have identified the "greatest hits," you need to challenge their validity. Is there any truth to the things your critic says? I often find that the critic has an ounce of truth in every two-pound bag of doubt. So extract the truth, take what you can learn from it, and throw the bag away without a second thought. Sometimes the narrative you build up in your head is worse than the reality of the situation.

Fellow keynote speaker and entrepreneur Jia Jiang conducted an incredible experiment that proved that oftentimes the narrative you tell yourself is worse than reality. Jia had a deep-rooted fear of rejection, a common manifestation of the inner critic. After a failed startup attempt, Jia decided to confront his fear directly in a bold experiment he called the "100 Days of Rejection." In an effort to desensitize himself to rejection and quiet his inner critic, he deliberately sought out rejection for 100 days by making outlandish requests of people. In often hilarious fashion, Jia made requests including the following:

- Asking a stranger to loan him $100
- Asking for a "burger refill" at a fast-food restaurant
- Asking to be a "Walmart-style" greeter at Starbucks
- Asking Krispy Kreme for Olympic ring–shaped donuts
- Asking a flight attendant if he could make an announcement over the loudspeaker
- Asking for a haircut at PetSmart

I would highly recommend his book, *Rejection Proof: How I Beat Fear and Became Invincible Through 100 Days of Rejection*, to find out what requests were successful. What Jia ultimately discovered was that the rejection wasn't as terrifying as his inner critic made it out to be. In fact, he was surprised by the number of people willing to say yes to his odd requests. This experiment was transformative for Jia, teaching him resilience, courage, and the ability to see rejection as an opportunity rather than a roadblock.

Reframing the Rants

The next step to crushing the critic is all about reframing negative thoughts into positive ones. Reframing is a powerful tool that can transform the way you view the world and yourself. It's a mental strategy for overcoming limiting beliefs perpetuated by your inner critic. Reframing starts by recognizing when your inner critic is getting in your ear, which is why I suggested you write down your critic's greatest hits earlier so that you can quickly recognize when this is happening.

Once you recognize the songs of self-doubt being sung to you, it's time to become a "bad interpreter." Let me explain. I want you to treat the negative thoughts as if they were a foreign language that needs interpreting, and *you* are the interpreter. Here's the fun part:

you don't speak the language! Ha! That means you can translate whatever that negative thought is to anything of your choosing.

Your inner critic decides to hit you with "You aren't good enough to do this." You consult your bad interpreter dictionary and reframe that thought as "It's really not even fair that I am being allowed to do this; I'm basically a professional." How fun is that?! By reframing whatever drivel that voice of doubt has to say into something powerfully encouraging, you crush the critic and take away all its power.

Take a Moment

Be a Bad Interpreter

Choose one of the negative thoughts from your Catch the Critic exercise. Put on your "bad interpreter" hat and translate it into its most ridiculously positive opposite.

The more you put this reframing technique into practice, the more resilient you become. By challenging and changing negative thought patterns, you build up your mental strength and adaptability. It's going to require some patience as it takes time to be consistent with reframing, but eventually, you will rewire your brain to default to positive affirmations rather than having to make a conscious effort. Taking control of your inner narrative gives you authority over your thoughts and emotions.

Your Critic-Crushing Crew

Sometimes, no matter what you try, you can't seem to quiet the voice of your inner critic. Even after trying to become a bad interpreter, your emotions are too strong, and you need help. In these isolated cases, I highly recommend assembling a

"Critic Crushing Crew" of a few devoted friends that you can call on at a moment's notice to help you overcome your fears. When you are putting together your crew, you should try to have three different personality types represented:

- **The Ass-Kicker:** The Ass-Kicker is the friend with tough love who knows just how to (not-so-gently) nudge you when you're stuck. They might not tell you what you want to hear, but they'll definitely tell you what you need to hear. The Ass-Kicker has a no-nonsense, straight-to-the-point attitude and will always be in your corner, cheering you on, pushing you forward, and taking your goals as seriously as you should. When your inner critic is holding you back, the Ass-Kicker will remind you of your goals and push you to meet them head-on, often with a dose of enthusiasm and energy that can reignite your drive.

- **The Coddler:** On the other hand, the Coddler is the friend who gives you comfort and empathy when you're too hard on yourself. This friend listens without judgment, offering a supportive shoulder when you need to lean on someone. They are good at helping you work through your emotions and reminding you of your many virtues and sometimes forgotten accomplishments. The Coddler encourages you to have the self-compassion needed to get through the tough times. Their warmth and lightness of touch can make the hard feelings you're experiencing a bit softer and easier to manage.

- **The Reasoner:** The Reasoner brings a balanced perspective to your Critic Crushing Crew. This friend is all about using the tools of logic and reason to help you take apart and understand the exaggerated claims your inner critic makes. They assist you in evaluating your fears and doubts objectively, often providing clarity and perspective to make those worries seem less big and bad. What does the Reasoner do? you could ask. The Reasoner helps you identify irrational thoughts and replace them with constructive ones.

Be Kind to Yourself

Some of the most compassionate people I know have a terrible time being kind to themselves. They can find more empathy watching a sappy, Sarah McLaughlin–scored, adopt-a-dog commercial than they can for their own lives. Crushing the critic requires self-compassion. You have to manage that unrelenting voice that pushes you over the edge. You can't let it sabotage your effort, fuel your self-doubt, or stop your personal growth. You have to be kind to yourself, be more understanding, and offer the same acceptance you would to a child who doesn't know better.

Imagine your best friend confides in you that they feel totally inadequate and useless. Would you mock them? Make them feel powerless? Call them names? Of course not! You would show them unconditional love and support. You would make them remember the incredible things they have already accomplished and point out all their strengths and the value they bring to the world. You would immediately recognize their suffering and meet it with uncompromising compassion.

This is the same approach you need to adopt for dealing with yourself. I don't know if you've ever been told this, but ...

YOU ARE NOT PERFECT...

no matter what your mother has told you.

Accepting yourself for the beautiful imperfection that you are is a non-negotiable. You are a work in progress. We all are. We learn, grow, make mistakes, and evolve.

Here are some ways to be a little kinder to yourself and build self-compassion:

- **Curate your emotional diet:** Just as you choose the right foods to eat, be mindful of the information and influences you consume. Try turning off Fox News, CNN, and MSNBC, and limit your exposure to negativity. Watch some powerful TED Talks or an inspiring movie or documentary. There is no room in your mental pantry for negative shit.

- **Capture the "yet"i:** Unlike the elusive sasquatch, capturing the power of "yet" is not only possible but can be a transforming experience. Try adding the word "yet" to the end of any self-criticism. "I'm not good at this ... yet." "I haven't accomplished what I wanted to ... yet." This is a powerful way to cultivate hope.
- **Establish a tiny reward rule:** Don't wait for some huge win to celebrate. Instead, give yourself tiny rewards for tiny wins. Buy that craft beer, that Whatchamacallit® bar, or those earrings at the checkout at the pharmacy. Tiny wins ... tiny rewards. It builds your self-worth and helps build momentum.
- **Spend time with your inner circle:** Surround yourself with the people who choose to love, uplift, and encourage you. The more positive influences you can expose yourself to, the more they balance out the negative self-talk.
- **Create a "Mistake Museum":** Instead of hiding your big mistakes, create a fun "museum" to display them. Write them down on pieces of paper, frame them, and hang them on the wall. When your friends come over, offer to walk them through your version of *Ripley's Believe It or Not!*®
- **Give your critic a name and silly voice:** My inner critic's name is Peggy, named after the girl who tortured me on the playground in elementary school. Peggy has a high, whiney voice that annoys most dogs within a 5-mile radius. She also has lice. It's my inner critic, and I decide what it looks and sounds like!

As a final thought, if you are struggling beyond what these suggestions are able to provide, you should think seriously about speaking to a mental health professional. Finding the right person to share your feelings with can be the most important piece to learning to deal with your inner critic and building the momentum to carry you toward your goals.

Moments to Remember:

- Your inner critic isn't a human flaw; it's part of the human condition.
- Your inner critic is designed to keep you safe and stop you from taking risks.
- Your inner critic comes from a cauldron of evolutionary instinct, social expectations, and personal experiences.
- Your inner critic is a master of disguise, adept at using various tactics to slow down your progress and stop momentum.
- The first step in outmaneuvering your inner critic is recognizing its patterns.
- The critic's narrative built up in your head is often worse than the reality of the situation.
- Sometimes you need the help of your Critic Crushing Crew to quiet your inner critic's voice.

9

BUMP the Moment: How to Instantly Create Momentum

Momentum Objectives:

- Learn the BUMP framework to build momentum.
- Discover how to create a sense of belonging.
- Foster a deeper level of understanding.
- Create a stronger sense of meaning.
- Understand how to connect to a larger purpose.

WE HAVE EXAMINED how letting go of fixed long-term plans can better position you to adapt to change and to take advantage of new opportunities. We have discussed how you have to use Moment Momentum to drive you closer to your goals. By being fully present and in the moment, you can focus and capture the opportunity directly in front of you. So how do you turn everyday moments into powerful momentum?

You need to BUMP the moment.

Think about the physics of a bump. Even the slightest bump transfers energy and alters the direction of both objects involved. BUMPing a moment is similar. It is a four-step process, grounded in behavioral science, that will help you infuse energy into every-day moments and shift their direction toward meaningful progress.

The Four Elements of BUMP

BUMP is an acronym for the four elements of human momentum: *Belonging, Understanding, Meaning,* and *Purpose.* We will discuss the individual importance of each of these elements, and then we will talk about the simplest form of applying them to create undeniable momentum.

Belonging

Building momentum is rarely a solo endeavor, so the journey toward unleashing momentum begins with building a sense of **belonging**. Psychologist Abraham Maslow called it a fundamental human need. We all want to feel like we belong. Belonging serves as the foundation for constructing meaningful connections and for identifying where authentic communication can flourish. When you feel like you belong, you feel seen, heard, and valued for who you are. Having a sense of safety and acceptance creates a fertile ground for growth, collaboration, and eventually transformation.

Why is belonging so crucial? Belonging has the power to do many things:

- **Dismantle defenses:** When you feel secure and accepted, you're more likely to let down your guard. This vulnerability is essential for genuine connection and allows you to be truly present in the moment.

- **Create a safe space:** A sense of belonging creates a circle of trust, where individuals feel comfortable sharing their thoughts, feelings, and ideas without fear of judgment or retaliation. This trust is needed for authentic communication and collaboration to thrive.
- **Empower risk-taking:** When you know you're supported and valued, you're more likely to step outside your comfort zone, embrace challenges, and pursue new possibilities. This willingness to take risks is often the catalyst for personal and collective growth.
- **Encourage accountability:** When you feel like you belong, you develop a shared sense of ownership. Feeling seen, heard, and valued fosters an accountability to own a shared goal. This sense of ownership can change behavior, encouraging a higher quality of work, a stronger commitment of time, and an emotional connection to success.

Creating a sense of belonging isn't about agreeing on everything or suppressing individuality. It's about fostering an environment of mutual respect, empathy, and genuine connection. It's about recognizing what everybody brings to the table and creating a space where everyone feels they can show up as their true selves. Belonging encourages a deeper level of vulnerability that can lead to transformative experiences.

The good news is that creating a sense of belonging isn't some mystical art reserved for social movements, hippies, and cult leaders. It's a skill that can be cultivated and applied in any moment, whether you're interacting with a loved one, collaborating with a colleague, or connecting with your audience online.

Here are several ways you can become more skilled at fostering a sense of belonging:

- **Practice engaged listening:** Focus on the speaker's message and ensure that you do not interrupt. Once they finish speaking, replace the initial message in your mind with what you've just heard. Then confirm you understood by reflecting the essence of their message back to them.

- **Push for lots of different viewpoints:** Make it possible for all kinds of people to express their opinions. Sometimes you just have to go around the room and allow people to say their piece.
- **Recognize contributions:** Value and appreciate the contributions that each individual brings to the table. Let them know that you see their efforts and that what they do matters.
- **Design for inclusivity:** Cultivate environments, whether physical or virtual, that are welcoming and accessible to all. Ensure that everyone feels comfortable and included.
- **Promote free expression:** Foster an open style of communication by modeling that style yourself. It is crucial for you to be as honest and transparent as possible. Make it evident that you respect all opinions—especially the ones that do not align with the majority.
- **Embrace empathy:** Embrace empathy by practicing it as a skill. Empathy helps to form deeper bonds and connections; most often, it yields a greater sense of trust. When you are in a situation of leading and trying to understand someone's perspective, it is helpful to imagine yourself in their position and think of how many different feelings and perspectives there might be.
- **Cherish differences:** Celebrate the diversity within your group. Host cultural appreciation days or encourage team members to share personal stories or traditions. Getting a better understanding of people's journeys helps to find shared values and experiences.
- **Provide risk support:** Offer help and encouragement when others are taking risks or facing challenges. Supporting others when they are sticking their necks out is a fantastic way to encourage creative and innovative solutions.

Protect Your Herd In a recent interview I conducted for my podcast, I learned about an incredible phenomenon from my dear friend and president/founder of ThinkLab, Amanda Schneider. She told me about a unique behavior in elephants. They have stunning family dynamics that are not entirely dissimilar to human ones and that last for generations. Elephants not only have a full range of emotions like humans but also have the ability to form a complex social structure that allows them to build an incredible sense of belonging. Scientists and nature photographers have documented a unique behavior within the elephant community called an "elephant circle." This behavior occurs only in two distinct scenarios.

The first is when a female elephant is about to give birth. The other females place themselves in a circle around her to protect the mother and her baby in this vulnerable state. When the calf is born, the females raise their trunks and trumpet in celebration.

The second time this behavior is exhibited is when a female elephant is injured. Once again, the females in the herd circle around the wounded elephant. This time they stomp their powerful feet to kick up dust. They do this to shield the distressed female's body and mask the pheromones coming off of her to protect her from potential predators nearby.

What can we learn about creating a sense of belonging from these elephants? In its rawest form, belonging is all about a feeling—an incredibly powerful feeling of connectedness. In this light, ask yourself, will you be the type of person who celebrates with your teammates when they do something amazing? Better yet, will you be the type of person to surround them and kick up a little dust to protect them when they need it? Saying yes to both of these questions will allow you to build a near-unbreakable sense of belonging.

Take a Moment

A Feelings Gut Check

In your next meeting with co-workers or in a discussion with a loved one, ask them how they are feeling about the current project or situation. Confirm that their feelings and experiences are legitimate and show that you see their perspective, even if you don't share it.

Understanding

Belonging lays the groundwork; it says, "I see you; I hear you; we're in this together." But to truly elevate a moment from ordinary to extraordinary, we need **understanding**—a bridge built not just on a shared presence but on a shared comprehension. Understanding goes beyond surface-level acknowledgments. It's about going deeper—grasping the nuances, the unspoken truths, and the other person's experiences. It's about seeing the world through their eyes, even if just for a moment.

Understanding has the power to elevate a moment as it:

- **Builds intimacy:** In both your personal and professional life, understanding helps you work through disagreements, support one another during rough times, and celebrate important moments together. It builds on the vulnerability that belonging encourages and strengthens the bond between you and others.
- **Builds bridges:** Understanding helps with the acceptance of different viewpoints and reduces the potential for unconscious bias. It helps build bridges between generations. When you understand the reasons behind someone's

thoughts or beliefs, you can establish empathy and reframe their input more constructively. Understanding improves overall teamwork, speeds up results, and bolsters company culture.

- **Amplifies self-awareness:** When you explore your own goals, motivations, and fears, you learn crucial information about yourself. This self-awareness helps you make better decisions and understand where to focus your time and efforts.

Establishing a sense of understanding is essential because it affirms people's inherent value and ensures they feel heard and respected. It goes beyond just recognizing someone's existence to acknowledging their unique perspectives and experiences. This deeper level of understanding builds trust and strengthens relationships, which sets the stage for more effective collaboration and communication.

During the Civil War, President Abraham Lincoln faced incredible pressure within his cabinet, which disagreed about almost everything. Rather than imposing a "my way or the highway" approach, he actively sought to understand the individual perspectives of his cabinet members. Even when speaking to those who strongly opposed his views, he engaged in deep conversations, showed empathy, and tried to find common ground. It wasn't easy, but he fostered a sense of shared understanding and was able to generate more effective decision-making during a critical period in American history.

You don't need to be Honest Abe to harness the power of understanding. You just have to be an active listener who wants to grasp another's perspective fully. When you create a reality rooted in shared comprehension, you unlock a deeper, more meaningful connection, paving the way to unstoppable momentum.

How can you create a deeper sense of understanding? The following suggestions can help:

- **Become an emotional listener:** Hearing a person's words is the simple part. It's much more challenging to understand the emotions and intentions behind those words. That's what emotional listening is all about—getting the whole message, not just the verbal part. You want to understand the feelings attached to the words.

- **Listen to understand:** Make it a routine to fully understand someone else's position before you launch into sharing your own. This might not seem like a huge deal, but at the speed of business, taking time to really understand someone can yield new insights into your own position and foster mutual respect.

- **Cultivate curiosity:** Channel your inner "Curious George" and engage in dialogue with a spirit of curiosity and an eagerness to understand. Remember that each person is unique, with a singular set of experiences that colors their viewpoint.

- **Embrace the awkwardness:** Allow conversations to be a little awkward. Don't be afraid of the silence in conversations. Sitting with discomfort and giving people a chance to think can produce more thoughtful responses.

- **Get clarity:** Achieving crystal-clear clarity may be one of the only times it is acceptable to over-communicate. Make sure everyone agrees on the details of whatever project you are working on. Speak the details; write the details; own the details. It's too easy to allow subjectivity to tank a project.

- **Offer your own experiences:** When the moment calls for it, relay to your people your own stories that connect with the subject matter. This can lead to a give-and-take atmosphere where understanding becomes mutual.

- **Acknowledge unspoken truths:** Pay attention to the nonverbal clues happening around you. If it's obvious that something is not sitting well with the team, call it out and address it. Bringing those emotions to the surface now can eliminate them biting you later.

- **Develop your emotional intelligence:** Make a concerted effort to recognize, understand, and direct the flow of your own emotions. Keeping your emotions in check and aligning them with the appropriate message can improve understanding and motivate others in the process.

Most of these suggestions offer ways to cultivate a deeper level of understanding, but sometimes the smallest detail can be your biggest undoing. Before moving on to the next element of momentum, let's highlight the particular importance of the "Get clarity" piece of understanding, as illustrated with an example from NASA.

NASA had a big goal of launching the Mars Climate Orbiter on December 11, 1998. Yet a small error in the details shared between teams led to disastrous results—a mission failure that might otherwise have been avoided. This project was a joint effort between NASA and Lockheed Martin. The mix-up is almost comical in retrospect, and it centers on a simple misunderstanding. Over the course of building the Orbiter, no one ventured to ask what unit of measure was going to be used for the propulsion calculations. The group at NASA's Jet Propulsion Laboratory (JPL) that was doing the calculating used the metric system, while the people at Lockheed Martin, who built the spacecraft, used the imperial system. The project's leadership apparently never noticed the two different teams using two different systems of measurement.

On September 23, 1999, as the Mars Climate Orbiter was getting close to Mars, the navigation error stemming from the unit mismatch caused the spacecraft to descend too steeply into the Martian atmosphere. It was either broken up in the atmosphere or sent off on a trajectory to nowhere. Either way, the orbiter was lost. The loss of the Mars Climate Orbiter was a $125 million setback for NASA.

Needless to say, the importance of getting clarity around the specifics of any project is paramount in creating momentum. Try not to let the desired speed of business make you overlook the important details that truly impact the project.

Take a Moment

In Your Words

In an upcoming conversation with someone, create a shared reality by reflecting back what you're hearing in your own words—not just repeating what you heard verbatim but capturing the essence of the moment.

Meaning

Belonging creates a dedicated team, and understanding builds a bridge of shared comprehension, but it's the activation of personal values that injects true **meaning**. In my last book, *Black Sheep: Unleash the Extraordinary, Awe-Inspiring, Undiscovered You*, I laid out the process of discovering your non-negotiable values. I called them your *Black Sheep Values*™. I was in my mid-40s before someone explained to me why farmers value black sheep differently than the rest of the flock. The real reason is because a black sheep's wool cannot be dyed. In effect, every black sheep is 100% authentically original and cannot be made into something it wasn't meant to be.

This explanation resonated deeply with me. At the time I was dealing with all of my son's medical drama and feeling like I could be pushed to believe or do anything, as I wasn't tethered to a set of non-negotiables that bring stability and keep you grounded. It sent me on a journey to discover those personal core values that would guide my decisions, set my moral compass, and define who I truly am.

When you are trying to build momentum, understanding your core values provides a profound sense of meaning that can be used to keep yourself motivated and committed to the process, allowing you to form more meaningful connections with those around you. Having clarity on these values also enables you to amplify your sense of belonging (connecting shared values) and understanding (sharing what matters most to you).

Discovering Your Non-negotiable Values   So how do you discover your non-negotiable values? I am going to make this as easy as possible for you. My company, Black Sheep Foundry, developed a free online assessment that helps you separate the things that are non-negotiable from the things that are merely "important." You can take the assessment by visiting DesigningMomentum .com and following the instructions there.

Once you have discovered your non-negotiable values, you can activate them. What I mean by this is you can speak them into existence, choosing when and where they appear. When trying to create momentum, you can decide which value will have more impact on moving things forward. Acting with deliberate intention—by choosing the specific value most relevant to the desired outcome—is how you create a deeper level of meaning and a stronger connection to the goal.

At Black Sheep Foundry, we have collected more than half a million data points with regard to personal values. If there was one "aha" moment that the data has revealed, it's that the number-one shared value among all humans is connection.

In fact, it's the number-one shared value by a 50% margin over the next closest shared value. This should tell you how desperately we all long for real connection.

Connection is firmly rooted in meaning. Think about your favorite sports franchise or recording artist. Sitting in a stadium or arena next to fellow fans creates an immediate connection that transcends social norms. Would you normally jump up and down and hug a stranger in celebration? Would you grab someone's hand you don't know and sing at the top of your lungs to them? That is the power of connection. It is charged with influential emotions!

Knowing that we all have an insatiable desire for connection, when we bring meaning to the table and explain "what truly matters to us," we give people something to connect to. It's a powerful way to discover shared values, channel the attached emotions, and build momentum together.

Meaning accelerates momentum as it:

- **Increases motivation:** Meaning provides a personal "why" and a stronger connection to the big goal. Internal motivation is far more powerful than external pressure.
- **Builds resilience:** You are far less likely to give up when you have a deeper sense of meaning attached to your efforts, which is essential for maintaining momentum.
- **Ignites inspiration:** When you are passionate and driven by meaning, you can inspire others to stretch beyond being comfortable and engage with more energy and commitment.

A League of Their Own   One of the most creative examples I have ever seen of infusing company values into a sense of meaning in the work they do is from a small, innovative nonprofit called Cannonball Kids cancer (CKc). I have long been an admirer and supporter of their groundbreaking work. CKc's mission is to fund innovative, accessible research for children fighting cancer to provide better treatments and quality of life and to educate for change.

At the time of publishing this book, CKc had invested nearly $4 million in pediatric cancer research, including creating almost 800 treatment options for children whose only other alternative was hospice. In 2023, CKc launched a truly innovative fundraising campaign called L.O.U.D.—The League Of Unstoppable Donors.

This "secret society" campaign consisted of printing beautiful, metal token coins with a message of "Official L.O.U.D. Business—Scan Immediately" on one side and a scannable QR code on the other. These coins were given to a small group of people with instructions to hand them to influential people they thought would be interested in becoming potential donors. This was a completely different strategy than the traditional big fundraising event. This was an intimate personal ask shrouded in mystery.

If you received a coin and scanned it, the QR code brought you into an interactive website that asked if you were ready to accept your mission. You were then taken on a journey, infused with meaning and facts about pediatric cancer, as well as information about your specific coin. You were told how many people had been invited to join this society, how many active states and countries these coins had traveled to, how many miles your specific coin had traveled, how many people your personal coin had been handed to, and how much money your coin and the campaign had raised.

You were then presented with a "Mission Critical" digital folder that contained the real meaning of the campaign: to raise $200,000 to fund a specific research grant. You were then asked to donate. By making this an exclusive interactive journey that you could follow along with and by injecting meaning into every stage of the journey, CKc was well on its way to accomplishing their goal.

Using their organizational values of innovation, creativity, and shared responsibility to drive the meaning behind this campaign was simply a brilliant way to let potential donors know about what matters most to the organization and give people a chance to connect in a completely unique way.

Take a Moment

A Value Reveal

In the next meeting at work or conversation with a friend, reveal a personal value related to the conversation. Give people a chance to connect on a deeper level with what truly matters to you. Keep it relevant and meaningful.

Purpose

You've constructed a sense of belonging, built bridges of understanding, and injected the power of meaning. Now it's time for the final, crucial step: connecting the moment to purpose.

Purpose, in relation to creating momentum, is the reason you are doing what you are doing. In this context, purpose becomes the big goal you are trying to achieve. However, it goes deeper than simply establishing a goal; it's about aligning your actions (next steps) with the big goal that gives your efforts direction and significance. It allows you to channel your efforts and values toward accomplishing a single goal.

Purpose moves the moment forward as it:

- **Creates intentionality:** Being intentional means choosing actions that align with your values. For example, if teamwork is one of your core values, attend meetings with the

specific intention of fostering collaboration. This deliberate focus turns passive participation into active engagement.

- **Ignites a call to action:** A shared purpose naturally generates a call to action. When everyone involved understands
the "why" behind their efforts, they are more motivated to
contribute and work toward a common goal. This shared
vision creates a cohesive and driven team dynamic.
- **Unites everyone:** Purpose fosters a sense of shared identity
and belonging. It reminds everyone that they are part of
something bigger than themselves, bringing people together
to strive for a common objective. This unity strengthens
bonds and enhances collective momentum.

Connecting to purpose is finding that natural alignment between
meaning, actions, and the potential momentum within a
moment. By linking actions to purpose, you transform a simple
interaction into a catalyst for tangible outcomes.

BUMP in Action

BUMP is a practical tool for unlocking the potential in any interaction. Now that you understand the four elements of human
momentum, let's break the elements down to the simplest, easy-
to-apply process for transforming moments into momentum.
When engaging in an everyday moment, apply the four steps of
BUMP by asking questions at each step:

1. **Belonging:** *Who belongs in this moment?*
   Asking this question strives to have every relevant
   voice related to the particular moment included. The
   goal here is to make sure that no stakeholders are left
   out of the conversation. Asking specific people to be a
   part of the moment indicates a perceived value they
   bring to the table, opening up the opportunity for unique
   contribution.

2. **Understanding:** *What are we trying to accomplish in this moment?*

   Clarifying the "what" creates a shared understanding of objectives, eliminating confusion and focusing energy on a common goal. A deeper level of understanding makes people feel heard and respected so you can build trust and strengthen relationships. Give everyone involved in the moment a chance to be heard. While diving deeper into understanding, take the opportunity to cover all the details to avoid any subjectivity.

3. **Meaning:** *Why are we trying to accomplish this?*

   Exploring the "why" connects the moment to personal values, injecting meaning and amplifying motivation. This is an opportunity to speak about what truly matters to you, giving others an opportunity to find points of connection in the values you hold dear. Creating a deeper level of meaning fosters a stronger level of accountability and commitment to achieving the goal.

4. **Purpose:** *What are the next steps toward reaching the desired outcome?*

   Remember, aligning your actions with the big goal gives your efforts direction and significance. Determining the next steps turns intention into action, creating tangible progress and building momentum.

Real-Life Example: Senoia Porchfest Music Festival

I recently participated in the Senoia Porchfest Music Festival in the small town of Senoia, Georgia. This is now an annual event as the inaugural festival in 2022 was a big success. Working closely with one the festival organizers, I was able to witness how the BUMP framework supported them in organizing and running a near-flawless event:

1. **Belonging:** *Who belongs in this moment?*

Scenario: The Senoia Downtown Development Authority organizes Senoia Porchfest each year. This incredible community music event features local and regional musicians performing on the residential porches of many of the historic homes in downtown Senoia, Georgia.

Identifying the key stakeholders: Who are the key stakeholders needed to make this event a success?

- *Musicians and bands:* Ranging from solo acts to full bands across various genres
- *Porch hosts:* Homeowners willing to provide their porches as stages
- *Vendors:* Food trucks, drink proprietors, and artists displaying their work
- *Volunteers:* Local residents/music lovers to help manage event logistics
- *Local business owners:* Downtown businesses involved in promoting the event
- *Local/regional press:* Print and online publications needed to promote the event in the region

2. **Understanding:** *What are we trying to accomplish in this moment?*

    Scenario: The goal of the festival is to create an engaging, community-driven event that celebrates music, creativity, and togetherness.

    Developing a greater level of understanding: There are hundreds of moving parts to successfully host a festival like this. Having a clear understanding of what you are trying to accomplish and what will be needed to do so is paramount. The following are some of the things that need clarification:

- Festival objective
- Attendee, band, vendor, volunteer experience
- Porch host requirements
- Vendor map
- Volunteer coordination

- Restroom facilities
- Power usage
- Street closures
- Police representatives
- Parking situation
- Audio/visual equipment
- Band participation
- Festival promotion
- Children's play area

3. **Meaning:** *Why are we trying to accomplish this?*

   Scenario: The Senoia Downtown Development Authority wants to foster community pride, celebrate local culture, and create lasting memories through the joy of music and art. They want to showcase the incredible talent in their own backyard.

   Developing a deeper level of meaning: A discussion to uncover the deeper reasons for hosting a community music festival is needed. What are the values that we want represented during this event? How can we create experiences to showcase those values? Some ways to show what they care about include:

   - *Senior golf cart transportation:* Providing transportation around the downtown area for older attendees can ease the pain of walking for miles to be able to experience the entire festival.
   - *Children's play area:* Creating a "kid only" play area can give parents a well-needed break over the course of a hectic day.
   - *Artist showcase:* Providing an area to showcase the work of local artists can foster a sense of belonging in the community.

4. **Purpose:** *What are the next steps toward reaching the desired outcome?*

Scenario: After setting the objectives, understanding the logistics and injecting a deeper meaning, it's time to plan the execution.

Identifying next steps: Undertaking a massive event with thousands of people can be overwhelming. It is crucial to focus one step at a time to move the event forward and give it the momentum you need to become a huge success. An event this size needs to break the "next step" into different categories to make it more manageable. These categories include the following:

- *Band handling:* Create a "band book" including the band schedule and their assigned porch selection, and provide materials for bands to help promote.
- *Event logistics:* You need a pre-event checklist, "day of" checklist, post-event checklist—you get the point. Breaking down logistics into bite-sized moments will help keep the momentum.
- *Promotion:* Create a social media schedule and contact local TV and radio channels to promote the event. Design "merch tents" to be placed around the event to sell merchandise.
- *Volunteer coordination:* Develop a volunteers' workshop to train them in what they will be responsible for during the event. Create a volunteer schedule to ensure you have enough coverage for the event.

By applying the BUMP framework, Senoia PorchFest was able to give itself the best opportunity to becoming a memorable event that not only showcases musical and artistic talent but also strengthens community ties and celebrates shared passions. This approach ensures that all voices are heard, objectives are clear, motivations are aligned, and actions are purposeful, creating an enriching experience for everyone involved.

Moments to Remember:

- BUMP is an acronym for the four elements of human momentum: belonging, understanding, meaning, and purpose.
- Momentum is rarely a solo endeavor.
- Belonging is the foundation of meaningful connection.
- Understanding creates a shared comprehension.
- Discovering your core values provides a deep sense of meaning.
- Connection is the number-one shared value among humans.
- Purpose is about aligning your actions with the big goal to give your efforts direction and significance.

10

Oversee the OGREs: Unleashing Emotionally Charged Moments for Maximum Impact

Momentum Objectives:

- Understand OGRE moments.
- Discover how to build emotional mass and momentum.
- Learn to maximize emotional velocity.
- Apply the BUMP framework to OGRE moments.

YOU LEARNED IN the previous chapter how the BUMP framework can create incremental momentum within any given moment; however, not all moments are created equal. Some moments are seething with an electric energy, a raw emotional charge that demands your attention. These are known as **OGRE** moments: moments with an Overwhelming Gut Reaction of Emotion attached to them. They can be positively exhilarating (when you land that dream job) or terrifying (when you receive that unwanted diagnosis), but they all have one thing in common: *intensity*.

115

This overwhelming gut reaction can cause a few significant changes:

Your beliefs can start shifting under your feet. Imagine standing on solid ground one moment, and the next, an OGRE is shaking the shit out of a flimsy rope bridge you are now standing on. The intensity of the moment can strip away any feelings of stability. You start to question everything. Your core beliefs—those bedrock values that shape your perception and decisions—begin to wobble. Suddenly, what you thought was certain is now up for debate.

In 1985, Steve Jobs experienced this himself when he was ousted from Apple, the company he co-founded. The boardroom coup, orchestrated by the very people he brought in, hurt him deeply. The belief of who he could trust shifted in an instant. This wasn't just a business setback; it was a blow to Jobs's core identity. The experience fueled a fire in him, a relentless drive to prove them wrong. It pushed him to create NeXT and Pixar, generating huge momentum and ultimately leading to his triumphant return to Apple. This OGRE moment of betrayal, though painful, became a catalyst for some of his greatest achievements.

Your thoughts can play a fierce game of mental tennis. When you get hit by an OGRE, your brain begins to panic and looks for a time in the past when you experienced something similar. Your brain wants to know what to do. If that wasn't enough, it also begins to forecast the future of what *could* happen after this moment is over. That moment can leave you feeling disoriented and unsure of your next move. An OGRE wants to send you into crisis mode and wreak havoc on your ability to function in the moment.

After 27 years of imprisonment by the apartheid regime, Nelson Mandela was about to walk out of prison and taste freedom for the first time in decades. But the emotional high he was on was at war with his thoughts. Mandela later reflected, "As I walked out the door toward the gate that would lead to my freedom, I knew if I didn't leave my bitterness and hatred behind, I'd still be in prison." Imagine the internal struggle: the years of suffering, the justified anger, battling against the hope for a better future and a nation healed. Mandela chose to harness this OGRE moment, lay down the weight of resentment, and catapult himself to the presidency of South Africa.

The Power of OGRE Moments: Building Emotional Mass

OGRE moments are intense and powerful. They hold the energy of being catalysts for change and could potentially drive a massive shift in momentum. But like any powerful force, they must be harnessed for you to benefit from them. Getting the most from OGRE moments requires a sensitive blend of emotional intelligence and strategic foresight. You're not just reacting to an amazing emotional experience; you're understanding the trajectory it has the potential to take. And you're using what you know about its emotional power to deliberately shape that trajectory into something with real, actionable momentum.

OGRE moments are meant to be shared. It's the sharing that amplifies the emotional energy, allowing you to build mass quickly and accelerate momentum. This "emotional momentum" is akin to the snowball effect, where the initial burst of emotion gathers more energy and followers as it rolls forward.

In the world of physics, momentum equals mass times velocity. Similarly, the same principle can apply to emotional momentum:

- **Mass:** Within the context of an OGRE moment, mass represents the number of people that an OGRE moment resonates with. It's the total *shared emotional energy*. Think of every viral video you have ever seen. These are perfect examples of an OGRE moment gaining mass as it resonated with millions of viewers. The more people who connect with the emotion, the greater the mass created.

- **Velocity:** Velocity represents the *direction* of the shared energy. It's about figuring out *where* and *with whom* to share the OGRE moment to generate maximum impact. When shared effectively, an OGRE moment can transcend its initial context, resonating with a broader audience who relate to its core emotional truth. This collective resonance not only validates the original experience but also multiplies its impact, creating a powerful wave of shared understanding and action. The act of sharing transforms an individual experience into a communal one, thereby magnifying its significance.

Do you remember the Nike ad "For Once, Don't Do it?" As a direct response to the chaotic scene around the death of George Floyd, Nike decided it was going to take a stand. In a twist on their iconic "Just Do It" mantra, they called out all the hatred, racism, and lack of accountability that was bubbling to the surface. The ad states, "Don't turn your back on racism. Don't accept innocent lives being taken from us. Don't make any more excuses. Don't think this doesn't affect you."

There was no mincing of words. Nike made the Black community and all those who were suffering feel seen, heard, and valued. They created a powerful sense of belonging. But they didn't stop there. They committed $40 million over four years to support the Black community in the United States by focusing on social justice, education, and economic empowerment. By publicly committing these resources and outlining their plan, Nike showed a true understanding of the need for real long-term solutions to systemic problems.

Nike's leadership shared personal stories and truths, adding authenticity and meaning to their message. They expanded that message to their substantial audience, encouraging everyone to take tangible actions toward change. They partnered with specific organizations and asked their customers to join them in supporting these causes.

Nike wasn't interested in a surface conversation about racial inequality; they wanted to start a movement. By aligning their values with significant action and sharing this OGRE moment with their customers, they grew their impact exponentially.

Finding Your Direction: Maximizing Emotional Velocity

Sharing an OGRE moment is required to create unstoppable momentum. However, you will need to be strategic about *where* and *with whom* you decide to share it with. You want to create maximum velocity.

- **Consider your audience:** Your audience matters. Understanding with whom you will find support is paramount. The same message shared with different communities can generate opposite results. Sharing a personal challenge with your "crew" can generate empathy and encouragement. Sharing that same message with "trolls" can lead to uncalled-for judgment and persecution.
- **Prioritize your platforms:** Choosing your vehicle for the distribution of your OGRE moment is a crucial step in generating momentum. Should you send an email? Make a phone call? Post on Instagram? Share in a private Facebook Group? The success of gathering mass will depend on you making the right decision.
- **Align with your purpose:** Blindly sharing without deliberate intention is like playing Russian roulette with your personal or organizational brand. Ask yourself, "What am I

trying to accomplish by sharing this OGRE moment? Is this about awareness? Action? Connection?" Let your purpose guide your direction.

Take a Moment

Hunt for OGREs

Take five minutes to reflect on the past week. List three moments where you experienced a strong emotional reaction (positive or negative). Briefly describe the situation and the emotion you felt. Which of these qualify as OGRE moments?

Bumping an OGRE

As powerful as OGRE moments are, they still need connection and direction. BUMPing an OGRE moment channels its intensity, amplifies it, and maximizes the potential momentum, as illustrated here:

- **Belonging:** Powerful emotions crave connection. By choosing the *right* audience and creating a sense of belonging, you better the odds of amplifying an OGRE's resonance.

  Example: Imagine the thrill of getting a promotion. Sharing this OGRE moment with your family and loved ones adds serious mass to the moment, multiplying the joy to be felt by all. Sharing the same promotion with the colleague who was passed over for the promotion … well … let's just say the only momentum built would be in their urge to raise their middle finger.

- **Understanding:** When emotions run high, clarity is even more important. Understanding will help you navigate the powerful surge of emotion, ensuring your OGRE moment propels you forward and not sideways. Understanding the potential impact of sharing, as well as what you are feeling in the moment, helps you choose the right direction and avoid unintended consequences.

Example: Consider the immense grief of losing a beloved pet. Sharing your OGRE moment with your fellow pet-loving community who understands the complexities of the bond between humans and animals can be a truly healing experience. However, posting raw emotions and unprocessed grief on social media can be a breeding ground for hateful comments leading to additional trauma.

- **Meaning:** Aligning your values with the OGRE moment will give it deeper meaning. The connection to a powerful "why" fuels the fire of your emotions, attracting others who share your values and amplifying the resonance of your moment.

  Example: Picture the deeply rooted passion of attending a rally for a cause you hold near and dear. Connecting your OGRE moment to your values of justice and equality magnifies the impact and alerts others as to what truly matters to you.

- **Purpose:** Connecting your OGRE moment to a larger meaning will transform your moment to movement. Purpose provides direction for turning your emotion into action, ensuring your emotional energy propels you toward your goals.

  Example: Think of the emotional toll of discovering that your favorite restaurant was being staffed by human trafficking victims. Connecting your OGRE moment to the purpose of raising awareness transforms your shock and frustration into action, creating a powerful impact that ripples out beyond your sole experience. This purpose-driven action becomes the spark of momentum toward a positive outcome.

BUMPing an OGRE moment is a powerful way to create unstoppable momentum. While your organization can learn to benefit from the intensity of these moments, one company took that concept to an entirely different level: GoPro.

GoPro is a company built on the idea of capturing and sharing OGRE moments. Their tiny cameras are designed to be used in scenarios that evoke strong emotions, like extreme sports. GoPro's success has come not from selling cameras but from selling the ability to document and share these incredibly powerful experiences.

GoPro has effectively turned the emotional power of OGRE moments into market momentum. Their strategy was brilliant:

- **Encourage and capture user-generated content (UGC):** GoPro empowers users to share their OGRE moments captured on their devices. By creating a massive library of content, they showcase the emotional power of their product. Their library becomes an ingenious marketing tool to inspire others to capture their own OGRE moments. They build *mass* through shared experience.
- **Harness social media:** Sharing users' OGRE moments creates endless viral videos seen by millions of people. The shareability of these moments creates velocity as the content is quickly consumed and spreads across platforms.
- **Become an OGRE-driven brand:** By associating themselves with these powerful moments, GoPro developed a strong emotional connection with their customers. People looking for a "camera" don't buy a GoPro. People who want that on-the-edge lifestyle of adventure and excitement buy GoPros. This deep connection fosters brand loyalty and drives sales.

Take a Moment

Transforming a Brand

Think about a brand that has effectively capitalized on an OGRE moment (like the Nike or GoPro examples in the chapter). Analyze their strategy. How did they build mass and velocity around the emotional moment? What can you learn from their approach?

The key to creating rocket-like momentum is capturing and harnessing OGRE moments. If you can learn to recognize these moments, you can learn to transform fleeting emotions into powerful action. Applying the BUMP framework and strategically sharing these moments with accepting audiences will unlock the potential for unstoppable momentum and extraordinary personal and professional growth.

Moments to Remember:

- OGRE moments have an Overwhelming Gut Reaction of Emotion attached to them.
- OGRE moments can cause your beliefs to shift and your mind to bounce between the past and present.
- Getting the most from OGRE moments requires a sensitive blend of emotional intelligence and strategic foresight.
- BUMPing an OGRE moment channels its intensity, amplifies it, and maximizes the potential momentum.

(*continued*)

(*continued*)

- OGRE moments are meant to be shared. Sharing amplifies the emotional energy, allowing you to build mass quickly and accelerate momentum.
- Within the context of an OGRE moment, *mass* represents the number of people that an OGRE moment resonates with.
- Within the context of an OGRE moment, *velocity* represents the direction of the shared energy.
- Being strategic about where and with whom you share your OGRE moment will maximize emotional velocity.

PART

III

The Ownership

11

Focus on Some "F" Words: Why Failure and Forgiveness Are Fundamental to Unstoppable Momentum

Momentum Objectives:

- Recognize the interplay between failure and forgiveness.
- Understand the role of failure in success.
- Reframe failure as feedback.
- Explore the dynamics of forgiveness.
- Learn the consequences of unforgiveness.

WHEN YOU THINK of the Rolls Royce of vacuum cleaners, only one name comes to mind: Dyson. The idea of paying $1,000 for a cordless vacuum seems almost ridiculous. But somehow, Dyson makes vacuums look ... well ... sexy. Their futuristic bagless curves and Dual Cyclone technology make them look like they'd be right at home on the *Enterprise* (Gen Z, that is a spaceship from the TV show *Star Trek* that debuted in 1966 ... are you keeping up?). You might think that the Dyson company had smoothly ascended the ranks of the household appliance industry, but you would be terribly mistaken.

James Dyson, the eccentric billionaire inventor, failed miserably before finding breakthrough success. In fact, he built more than 5,000 prototypes over the course of 15 years before he perfected his technology. Have you ever failed 5,000 times trying to accomplish a single endeavor? How many failures constitute … failure?

Dyson could have easily cashed in his chips and succumbed to resentment and bitterness. He could have blamed himself or the industry for the 15 years of struggle. But he chose a different path. He chose forgiveness. He forgave himself for all the questionable decisions, forgave the industry for its sorrowful lack of vision, and focused all his energy on learning from each experience. This radical forgiveness, along with his relentless pursuit of his idea, allowed him to persevere and build unstoppable momentum—momentum that led him to more than $7 billion in revenue in 2023 alone! That doesn't suck … get it? Thank you … I'll be here all week … try the veal.

Momentum is rarely a silky, smooth, uninterrupted process. It's a series of positive and negative moments filled with twists, turns, obstacles, and OGREs. It's more of a tango than a straight line to success. You have learned how the raw power of OGRE moments can be harnessed to generate extraordinary momentum. But what happens when your momentum stalls? What happens when you get knocked on your ass, make foolish mistakes, or find yourself stuck in a "Woe is me" cycle?

You need to get back to the fundamentals. Embracing failure and forgiveness is fundamental to maintaining any type of momentum. Failure is not a sign of weakness but a necessary catalyst for moving forward; and practicing forgiveness, for both ourselves and others, can free you from the emotional baggage that can stop you in your tracks.

The Tango of Failure and Forgiveness

Anyone who has danced the tango knows it demands a dramatic, closely knit partnership filled with complicated footwork and improvisation. Much of the same could be said about the interplay of *failure* and *forgiveness*. They are intricately intertwined along your journey toward personal growth and unstoppable momentum.

Failure becomes a powerful stimulant for transformation when coupled with the chain-breaking act of forgiveness. It creates a dynamic cycle where failure provides the opportunity for growth, and forgiveness provides the freedom to embrace that growth. When you experience failure, your first response is usually to place blame. You blame yourself, others, the situation, your hair, Obama ... you get it. Here's the thing:

Blame is an anchor, and anchors stop momentum.

Forgiveness reels the anchor in and lets you sail toward your goal. It allows you to navigate the interpersonal failures within a team or organization. When a project fails, team members often start pointing fingers at each other like they're Will Ferrell in *A Night at the Roxbury*. This creates a toxic environment that stops both collaboration and progress. However, if you foster a culture of forgiveness, where failure is expected and planned for, then it's viewed as just another step in the process toward reaching the goal.

The dancing duo of failure and forgiveness can also build exceptional resilience. When you aren't afraid of failure, you build the confidence to take more risks and become more innovative, as a setback becomes nothing more than a chance to gather additional information to recalibrate and move forward. Forgiveness prevents you from becoming trapped in a cycle of blame and negativity.

Building momentum isn't a straight line across the dance floor. Learning to dance the zig-zag pattern of failure and forgiveness makes you nimble-footed and able to work around the obstacles and challenges of uncertainty. It all begins with embracing failure.

Reframing Failure

Somewhere in the doldrums of history, we decided that failure was a bad thing, something to be avoided at all costs. Failure brings shame, embarrassment, and a feeling of being "less than." Failure makes you want to play it safe and stand back from the edge of risk and uncertainty. It doesn't have to.

What if you reframed your understanding of failure? What if it wasn't an "end" but a planned part of the process? A simple step on the path to success. If you think about it, failure is nothing more than feedback. It's an opportunity to gather information, make better-informed decisions, and adapt and refine your approach to your goals.

Thomas Edison said it best, "I have not failed. I've just found 10,000 ways it won't work." Thank goodness he did, or you'd be reading this book by candlelight.

Embracing Your Failures

Embracing your failures is important because it can change your perspective on growth and success. When you see failure as a normal and even valuable part of the learning process, you are more likely to view success as something that involves learning from mistakes rather than just not making mistakes. This shift in perspective encourages resilience—a sense that you can "bounce forward" from setbacks and keep building momentum.

Here are several ways to embrace failure:

- **Adopt a WITWAW mindset:** Believing that there is a way to move forward, even in the face of obstacles and failure, allows you to approach challenges with curiosity rather than fear. Instead of being paralyzed by doubt, you welcome failure, as the crucial information it provides moves you one step further to finding a way and achieving success.

- **Reframe failure as feedback:** View failure not as an end point but as a form of feedback. It provides the information you need to make better decisions and adjust your approach to achieving the big goal. This mindset allows you to see failure as a planned step on the path to success rather than a setback.

- **Write a failure résumé:** Create a résumé centered around all of your failures. List the jobs you didn't get, the potential soulmate that got away, the projects that fell short, and other setbacks you've experienced. This exercise can help you acknowledge how resilient you have been. Seeing how many times you have gotten up and brushed yourself off after being knocked down will help you temper the fear of failure.

- **Create a truly bad piece of art:** Have some fun and channel your inner Michelangelo to make an intentionally bad piece of art. The idea is that "failure" is a matter of perspective. While you might think the artwork is hideous, someone else will find it irreplaceable and priceless.

Embracing failure is a non-negotiable for any entrepreneur. Consider the story of Sara Blakely, the founder of Spanx. Sara faced numerous failures throughout her life. Whether it be unsuccessfully selling fax machines door-to-door, failing the LSAT twice, or being rejected to play Goofy at Disney World (too short), she was no stranger to failure. When Sara developed the idea for Spanx, she was consistently rejected by hosiery mills that didn't understand or believe in her product. She persevered until she found a single mill to take a chance on her. Sara had to self-fund her idea as financial backers wouldn't give her any money. She even had to walk into stores and personally demonstrate the product to show how her revolutionary idea worked. No matter the obstacle, she never gave up. Sara viewed every failure as important information she could use to pivot and refine her product and sales strategy. Fast-forward 20 years, and Sara sold Spanx for more than $1 billion.

Take a Moment

Reframing Failure

Reflect on a past failure in your own life. Don't dwell on the negative emotions, but instead ask yourself: What did I learn from this failure? What could I have done differently? How can I apply these lessons to a future failure?

Reframing Failure Example: From Malfunction to Momentum

To bring this concept closer to home, let's say your boss asked you to do an important presentation to a potential client. You spend weeks preparing, you channel your inner graphic designer on Canva, and you develop the most beautiful PowerPoint presentation you have ever seen. You rehearse every detail, building a compelling narrative that leaves only one decision the client could make. On the day of the presentation, the laptop malfunctions sending your slides out of order, breaking your concentration, and destroying the carefully crafted narrative you created. The presentation is a disaster and sends you into a tailspin. The client isn't impressed and decides to pass.

You feel like a failure. You hide in your office and replay the moment repeatedly in your head to punish yourself for the horrendous job you did. Your boss sees you struggling, sits down in front of you, and says, "I know you are disappointed, but let's not focus on that right now. Let's analyze the situation objectively." Together, you go through what went wrong and come up with some strategies to overcome the unexpected disruptions. You decide you should have a backup copy of the presentation on a thumb drive to be able to use someone else's computer in the event of a catastrophe, and you determine you should take a public speaking course to learn how to deal with challenges in real time. You realize that the "failure" wasn't a reflection of your competence but rather a specific moment with valuable lessons to be learned. There will be another opportunity to present to another client, except this time you will be even more prepared.

Several weeks go by, and another opportunity is on the calendar. You approach the presentation day with newfound confidence as the online public speaking course you took delivered key tactics to overcome any obstacle and you have not one but two thumb drives with copies of the presentation. You fire up the laptop, and even though there were some bumps along the way, you deliver a fantastic presentation that earns you a new client.

By shifting your perspective on failure, you were able to receive essential feedback and develop new skills to better prepare yourself for the future. By asking yourself, "What if there was a way to not let this happen again?" you used your curiosity to push forward and overcome every obstacle in your path—that is the power of reframing failure.

The Necessity of Forgiveness

While it may not be your favorite "F" word, you will have to learn to appreciate and embrace *forgiveness*. I hate that this word is mostly tied to religion. In the context of momentum, forgiveness isn't about your salvation; it's about releasing the incredibly heavy burden of resentment that simply stops any potential forward progress. Forgiveness is a courageous act of deliberate intention that breaks the chains of unresolved hurt, replacing the bitterness of resentment with an untapped well of renewed hope.

Forgiveness is not a powerless passive act; it is a direct confrontation of your own pain. You must think of forgiveness as a process of navigating complex emotions, not as a peaceful fantasy destination. Forgiveness is often a team sport. It may require reaching out to get some support from trusted friends and advisors or seeking out professional guidance. Unfortunately, there isn't a one-size-fits-all approach to forgiveness, but the benefits are undeniable.

Choosing to forgive releases you from your private personal prison and sparks a host of possibilities:

- **Unforeseen healing:** You begin to heal from past hurts you didn't even know you had. You start approaching each day with a lighter heart that creates space for powerful positive emotions like empathy, compassion, and connection. You begin to desire momentum.
- **Bridge-building:** You begin to mend broken relationships and strengthen existing ones. Forgiveness fosters a deeper trust and understanding that brings you closer together. The stronger your relationships, the stronger your momentum.
- **Self-awareness:** The deep personal reflection that forgiveness requires allows for a better understanding of what matters most to you and gives you a clearer picture of the person you long to be. This becomes powerful motivation to move forward.
- **Freedom:** When you break the shackles of the past, you find yourself standing in the present, which happens to be the only place to make positive changes, build momentum, and influence the future.

When you choose to forgive yourself and others, you become healthier and more optimistic, like someone who's tapped into a deeper understanding of life. The path to forgiveness is the path to understanding our flawed humanity. When you forgive, you are (no surprise here) more kind to yourself. And by "kind" I don't mean some cheerleader-like encouragement, "You can do it!" Instead, I'm talking about a truly admirable quality of which we can all partake: an empathetic understanding of our shared human condition. Forgiveness is by no means an easy task. You do it when you can, even though you are always working on that "can" part.

Take a Moment

An Act of Forgiveness

Think of someone who you are holding a grudge against. What is it that is stopping you from forgiving them? Can you accept what you can't change and find a way to release this burden by forgiving them? Write a short message expressing your forgiveness and put it away. Someday, when you are ready, send them the message and let go of the bitterness.

The Devastating Ripple Effect of Unforgiveness

When you hold on to resentment for yourself or others, it permeates almost every aspect of your life:

- **Your mental and emotional state:** Unforgiveness breeds negativity. It fuels stress, anxiety, and depression. It will consume your thoughts, distracting you from the present moment and taking away any opportunity for you to experience joy and peace. It's hard to move forward when your negativity influences your belief in what can happen.

- **Your relationships:** Holding grudges is toxic. It will poison your relationships with conflict and bitterness. Grudges bleed into "healthy" relationships and begin to make you distrust everyone and everything, killing any chance of momentum.
- **Your physical health:** There have been countless studies linking unforgiveness to heart issues and immune system problems. It literally weakens your defense systems, opening you up to a litany of health concerns. When you don't feel good, you don't want to do anything ... including building momentum.
- **Your personal growth:** You become so preoccupied with resentment you stop going after what you want. Your lack of focus clouds your judgment, limits your creativity, and prevents you from reaching your true potential.

When you choose to hold on to unforgiveness, you become an unhealthy, negative relationship-killing basket case going nowhere. Just the type of person your mother always hoped you'd be! Come on, you can do better.

Moments to Remember:
- Momentum is more of a tango than a straight line to success.
- Embracing failure and forgiveness is fundamental to maintaining any type of momentum.
- Failure is not a sign of weakness but a necessary catalyst for moving forward.
- Forgiveness, for both ourselves and others, can free you from the emotional baggage that can stop you in your tracks.

- Failure becomes a powerful stimulant for transformation when coupled with the chain-breaking act of forgiveness.
- Blame is an anchor. Anchors stop momentum.
- Forgiveness reels the anchor in and lets you sail toward your goal.
- Embracing failure can change your perspective on growth and success.
- Unforgiveness breeds negativity and fuels stress, anxiety, and depression.

12

Fire the Fortune Teller: The Future Is a Present Creation

Momentum Objectives:

- Develop a Moment Blueprint.
- Learn to set clear objectives.
- Create an optimal environment for your designed moment.
- Build connection through values.
- Plan for future actions.

IN THE PREVIOUS chapter, you examined the real power of embracing failure and forgiveness as fundamental steps toward maintaining momentum. You discovered how to reframe failure as crucial feedback and how forgiveness reels in the anchor holding you back, freeing you to propel yourself forward. You learned to tango with failure and forgiveness in order to fuel your personal growth. But what if you could become a choreographer of this dance? What if there was a way you could design moments to contribute to your momentum rather than reacting to whatever life throws at you?

If you treat your future as something left to the cards of a side-show fortune teller, the probability of you building momentum and achieving your big goals is left to chance. Are you comfortable with that? Write this down:

The future is a present creation.

More specifically, YOUR future is something YOU design through the intentional creation of present moments. You need to think of yourself as an architect who is meticulously designing the blueprint for your own momentum. Just as James Dyson designed more than 5,000 prototypes before perfecting his futuristic vacuum cleaner, you too can design specific moments that will lead to your success. That is what Moment Momentum is all about.

Designing a Moment Blueprint

You've learned about the BUMP framework and how it can create momentum within a moment, and you will use that during the actual moment itself. But now you need to shift your focus to proactive design—consciously creating the moments you want to happen. This shift in focus involves some forethought, planning, and intentionality.

Before getting into any specific strategies, you need to learn how to design a Moment Blueprint. A Moment Blueprint isn't a rigid script; it is more of a flexible framework that guides your actions. It consists of four different elements: the objective, the environment, the connection, and the future. It's the planning stage of designing momentum. When you strip it down to its simplest form, the designed Moment Blueprint addresses the following questions:

1. What is the objective of the moment you are designing?
2. Where should this moment take place?
3. What values are you going to lead and connect with?
4. What are the next steps to achieve the objective?

Let's break down each of the elements a little further to help you understand the context and how to use these elements to create a powerful moment of momentum.

The Objective: The Heart of Your Moment

When designing a moment, *defining your objective* is paramount to making it a success. It will serve as the compass that will guide your actions. This first step demands your full attention, as there is no room for any subjectivity on the matter. A clearly defined objective allows for complete alignment with it.

What is the specific outcome you want to see from this moment? What is the tangible change that you want to create? Are you trying to spark some innovation within your team? Are you trying to strengthen a bond with a loved one? Maybe you want to drive interest in your brand, capturing the attention of potential customers with the hopes of converting them into new clients. Or perhaps you are on a mission to mend a broken relationship to rebuild trust.

Whatever your objective, you need to articulate it with as much detail as you can. Rather than framing your objective as a subjective result, such as "have a productive meeting," drill down to something concrete like "come up with three possible solutions to problem X." The more specific your objective, the more effectively you can design a moment to achieve it.

Take a look at the following examples of objectives with possible strategies to articulate them:

- *Objective: to motivate a disengaged team*
    - You design an off-site retreat to allow your team to connect and rediscover their shared purpose through thoughtfully crafted moments on the agenda.
    - You plan a team-building activity that focuses on moments of collaboration that can rekindle some enthusiasm and rebuild teamwork.

- *Objective: to resolve a long-standing conflict with a family member*
  - o You schedule a private meeting in a quiet, neutral setting to air out your concerns. Through open communication and listening to understand rather than to respond, you focus on a desired outcome of mutual respect and a renewed commitment to repairing your relationship.
- *Objective: to generate 10 social media posts about an upcoming product launch*
  - o You organize a pre-launch event and invite 20 social media influencers so you can showcase your product's unique features and benefits and build some buzz around the launch.

These examples illustrate the importance of a clear objective. Each one has different levels of detail within them, from something that is more "big picture" like "motivation" to something incredibly specific like 10 social media posts. The latter has the ability to be tracked and monitored much more easily. The more you can tie the objective to measurable outcomes, the better chance you have of obtaining more data to inform your future actions. It's in the clarity of the objective that you begin to transform the future from a fortune teller's hogwash into a powerful present creation that shapes your reality one intentionally crafted moment at a time.

Hitting the Nail on the Head   Marty Dodson is a Nashville-based songwriter with 10 number-one hits to his credit. He has written songs for Blake Shelton, Carrie Underwood, Billy Currington, Kenny Chesney, Rascal Flatts, Big and Rich, Joe Cocker, and The Plain White T's, to name a few. Marty's journey to becoming a powerhouse song machine started off with years of dedicated effort with not much to show for it.

After two years of writing daily, with none of his songs being picked up to be recorded by an artist, a friend from church invited him out to lunch. Little did Marty know, but this was an intervention of sorts. The gentleman looked across the table at Marty and said, "I see that you've been doing the songwriting thing for a couple of years now, and nothing has happened. I wonder if I could offer you a job at my company." Facing the reality of his situation, Marty heard his friend out. "The job is writing instruction manuals for small appliances. You're a writer; you'd be great at it."

The salary for the job was more than Marty had ever made. It had full benefits and a retirement package. It was tempting, but as Marty tells it, "I went home and thought about it, and I thought, you know what? This will kill my soul. I don't want to write instruction manuals for small appliances. You know, that's not why I got into the writing stuff in the first place. So I called him up and thanked him, and told him no. And he kind of acted like I was crazy."

What Marty did next was an ingenious way of reminding himself of the objective he was about to set for himself. He hammered a single nail into the wall at the end of his hallway. That nail would stay empty until he achieved his objective of earning his first gold record.

As Marty remembers, "Every single day when I saw that nail, it was a reminder of that on this day, when you told this guy no, you believed you could do this."

The empty nail helped Marty stay focused on his objective and he kept writing day in and day out. He wrote hundreds of songs and danced the tango with failure and forgiveness for what seemed like forever. But four years after he designed a moment by hammering that nail into the wall, Marty got to hang his first gold record.

Setting a clear objective with measurable results helped build the incredible momentum that has carried Marty to the top of the country music scene and made him one of the most successful songwriters in the game. The actions that Marty took to achieve his goal were extremely deliberate, including the location of the nail in the hallway, where he knew he would see it every day. As we will discuss next, using your environment is a powerful way to help build momentum.

Take a Moment

Objective of Your Desire

Choose a personal or professional goal you want to achieve. Clearly define the specific outcome you want from a moment related to this goal. Write it down as concretely as possible.

The Environment: The Set Design for Your Moment

When choosing an environment for your designed moment, it's important to remember that the environment is more than simply a backdrop. The environment is an influential force that can either amplify or diminish the moment's impact. Just as a playwright anguishes over the set design for scenes, you have to think through how the environment will influence the experience you are trying to create. You will need to consider both the physical location and the atmosphere you want to cultivate.

Location, Location, Location　Where your designed moment takes place plays an important role in shaping its energy and outcome. A team-oriented brainstorming session might thrive in a bright, open space filled with natural light, while a sensitive conversation might be more well-suited to a more private and intimate setting.

Consider the following types of environments:

- **Stimulating environments:** If your moment requires creativity and innovation, opt for environments that spark inspiration such as a bustling shared workspace, a vibrant coffee shop, or even a busy restaurant. Surround yourself with things that ignite your imagination and encourage new ideas to flow.
- **Focused environments:** If your moment demands concentration and a deeper level of work, choose a quiet and distraction-free space such as a tucked-away conference room, a dedicated home office, or even a library. (Does anyone still go to the library?) No matter what, minimize the interruptions and create a space conducive to focus.
- **Relaxing environments:** For moments where connection and rejuvenation are the top desires, select a calming and more comfortable setting—perhaps a cozy living room, a beautiful park, or maybe a quiet space on a lake. Find a space that promotes relaxation and encourages people to unplug and unwind.

Atmosphere   Once you have chosen the perfect location, you need to think about the atmosphere or vibe you are trying to create. While it isn't something that most people think through, outside of something like a romantic dinner for two, the atmosphere is responsible for setting the emotional tone of your moment.

Think through the following atmosphere/vibe factors:

- **Lighting:** Soft, warm light creates intimacy and relaxation, while bright, cool light promotes focus and attentiveness. Holding your high-energy sales meeting in a dimly lit restaurant might not generate the excitement you are looking for. Make sense?

- **Music:** They don't call music the universal language for nothing. Music has a profound effect on mood and energy. You need to become your own personal DJ and choose music that reflects the atmosphere and desired objective. Do you need some calming smooth jazz in the background or do you need the Black Eyed Peas to "Pump It" and get everyone on their feet? Become a music matchmaker and watch how you can control your moment's mood.

- **Scents:** How many houses have been sold by the smell of fresh-baked cookies during an open house? Aromas can evoke powerful memories and emotions. There is a reason that the high-end hotels pump Palo Santo through their air vents. It makes their properties even *smell* expensive. Think through what scents can elevate your moment toward your desired outcome. Is it candles and oils? Coffee and pastries? Pizza and beer? Find your scent and let their noses pull them to your moment.

- **Visuals:** The visual elements of your environment can also influence the mood. An entire industry is built on "color theory" and how certain colors can affect how you feel. Think about artwork, plants, and even sparse or busy design. The visual will make people feel a certain way. You need to make sure that the visual you select aligns with the moment you are designing.

If you carefully consider location and atmosphere, you can craft an environment that powerfully supports your objective. The environment will help shape your experience and become an active participant in your moment design, helping to maximize your moment's impact. This attention to detail will elevate your moment from ordinary to extraordinary, generating the type of momentum that will propel you forward toward your big goals.

Take a Moment

Set the Mood

Identify a moment you want to create and describe the ideal environment for it. Think about the location, atmosphere, and other sensory elements (sights, smells, sounds, etc.) that would best support your moment. Write out a plan for setting up the environment.

The Connection: A Values-Forward Approach

Connection isn't only the number-one shared value among all people; it is also the dynamic exchange that lifts moments from being transactional to being transformative. Leading with your values creates a kind of "connection docking station" that others can plug into. When you connect through shared values, it becomes much easier to align your actions to your goal. Think of leading with your values as speaking them into existence. You choose when and where they appear to give others an opportunity to "dock" into them. When you are creating a moment, you want to try to create the strongest connection possible. The stronger the connection, the deeper the sense of belonging, understanding, meaning, and purpose—all of which are needed to BUMP a moment forward and create momentum.

Activating Your Values You have already learned the importance of figuring out your non-negotiable values, and once again, this deeper understanding of what matters most to you proves to be a crucial step as connection requires you to activate those values.

When trying to create deeper connection, consider the following:

- **Being transparent:** When you openly communicate your values and intentions, you create a deeper level of understanding and meaning that can become powerful motivators in your designed moment.
- **Walk the talk:** Your actions should be a direct reflection of your values. Don't profess one thing and act in an opposite manner. When you align your words and actions, you create a potent sense of authenticity that truly resonates with others.
- **R-E-S-P-E-C-T:** Take a lesson from Aretha and treat others with respect. Even when you don't share someone else's values, you still need to respect their values. As long as you have respect, you can disagree and still find potential ways to create momentum.

From Transaction to Transformation　Connection is the secret to converting moments from transactional exchanges to transformational experiences. When you feel connected, you have a stronger level of commitment to helping reach a desired goal. The presence of shared values and deeper meaning can infuse your moment with a shared sense of purpose and possibility.

Consider the following to elevate your moment to becoming transformational:

- **Plan time to celebrate:** As you are designing your moment to build momentum, plan time to celebrate with those who are involved when you accomplish your objective. Grabbing a celebratory drink or simply sharing a high-five can do wonders for strengthening bonds.
- **Plan on offering support:** Offer the necessary support based on the potential challenges your designed moment

might create. This plan will foster a strong sense of belonging, build resilience, and help maintain momentum.

■ **Plan for collaboration:** Planning for others to share in your moment will encourage them to take ownership of their role within it. Have several ideas of how someone can take responsibility so you can give clear direction as to what your expectations are. Momentum happens much faster when it's a team sport.

Take a Moment

A Values Docking Station

Identify two or three of your non-negotiable values and consider how they could be activated in a specific moment. Plan a small interaction where you can lead with these values and give people an opportunity to connect with you on a deeper level.

The Future: What Happens Next

When you are designing your moment, you should plan for what happens after the moment passes. Just as the BUMP framework ends with aligning actions and values to create intentional next steps, designing your moment requires you to think about what should happen next to ensure you build momentum.

From Potential to Kinetic   If you are going to build unstoppable momentum, you need to convert thoughts into actions. This involves thinking through all potential outcomes of your designed moment and having a plan for whatever direction it takes. Here are some important things to consider:

- **Identify actionable next steps:** Having small, achievable next steps planned out will make the objective less daunting and create a clear path for others to accept accountability for their roles.
- **Assign ownership:** Clearly define who is responsible for what. This clarity will ensure accountability, make it easy to track progress, and prevent tasks from falling through the cracks.
- **Establish deadlines:** Assigning tasks to people without establishing deadlines is a recipe for stalled momentum. Set realistic deadlines and an overall timeline for accomplishing the objective.

Sustaining Momentum   Once the momentum has started, you need to have a plan for sustaining it. This plan requires ongoing effort and attention, as momentum is not a one-time event but a continuous process. Plan on the following:

- **Schedule regular check-ins:** Establish a cadence of regular check-ins to review progress, address any concerns, and plan pivots where necessary. When you are using moments to drive momentum, you can be nimble in your approach to achieving the objective.
- **Embrace adaptability:** Be prepared to bob, weave, twist, and turn with uncertainty. Being flexible is essential for maintaining momentum.
- **Remember to recharge:** Build in time to rest and recharge to prevent burnout and to have the energy to sustain momentum. Building momentum can be exhausting as it ebbs and flows.

> **Take a Moment**
>
> **Future Planning**
>
> After designing a moment, outline the next steps you need to take to sustain momentum. Assign tasks to yourself and others, set deadlines, and track your progress.

Moment Blueprint Example: Team Innovation

Let's take a look at what a Moment Blueprint might look like for a Team Innovation session at work:

Objective
- **Specific outcome:** Inspire creative thinking and develop three innovative solutions for improving customer service experiences within the next quarter.
- **Tangible change:** Generate actionable ideas that enhance customer satisfaction and streamline service processes.

Environment
- **Location:** A bright and open co-working space with lots of natural light, conducive for creativity
- **Atmosphere:** Energizing and collaborative, with breakout areas for small group discussions
- **Vibe Factors:**
  - **Lighting:** Use of adjustable lighting to create a dynamic environment
  - **Music:** Upbeat instrumental playlists to maintain high energy without distraction
  - **Visuals:** Inspirational quotes and customer feedback displayed around the room to focus the team on the customer experience

Connection
- **Values activation:**
  - **Transparency and innovation:** Share your personal values and how they influence your ideas and suggestions. Encourage all team members to do the same. Explain you are looking for unique contribution and a deeper understanding of what matters most to everyone involved.
  - **Respect:** Encourage all team members to share ideas without judgment to foster a safe space for creativity.
  - **Collaboration:** Design exercises that require team members to build on each other's ideas.

Future
- **Actionable next steps:**
  - Schedule follow-up meetings to develop detailed project plans for the top three ideas.
  - Assign team leaders to champion each project idea and establish small teams for execution.
  - Set deadlines for initial project milestones and regular check-ins to ensure momentum is maintained.

By understanding the elements of the Moment Blueprint, you can craft powerful moments that set you up perfectly to use the BUMP framework. Having a clear objective will help you avoid confusion during the Understanding section of BUMP. Thinking through the environment of your moment and using your values to provide points of connection can help create a stronger sense of belonging and meaning. Finally, having the next steps already planned for the future builds a bridge to a shared purpose and converts the moment into action.

Ultimately, the combination of capturing moments as the universe provides them and creating moments of your own design provides you with the most opportunities to create momentum. It also allows you to take an active role in making sure these moments happen rather than waiting for them to be handed to you.

Moments to Remember:

- The future is a present creation.
- *Your* future is something *you* design through the intentional creation of present moments.
- A Moment Blueprint is created in the planning stage of designing momentum. It consists of four different elements: the objective, the environment, the connection, and the future.
- A clearly defined objective allows for complete alignment with it.
- The environment is more than simply a backdrop; it's an influential force that can either amplify or diminish a moment's impact.
- Leading with your values creates a kind of "connection docking station" that others can plug into.
- If you are going to build unstoppable momentum, you need to convert thoughts into actions.

13

Own Your Moment: Taking Accountability and Ownership Over Your Actions

Momentum Objectives:

- Discover the foundation of ownership.
- Identify strategies for building accountability.
- Learn to overcome accountability obstacles.
- Understand the ripple effect of ownership.

IN THE PREVIOUS chapter, you explored the art of designing a moment and how to elevate it from a transactional exchange to a transformational experience. You learned how to set clear objectives; cultivate a powerful environment; form deeper, more meaningful connections; and plan future steps to sustain momentum. But if you want to convert intention into actual progress, there is still one pivotal ingredient missing: *ownership*. It connects your aspirations to your actions.

Ownership is the bridge between dreaming and doing.

You might think that ownership is about taking control, but it's really about taking responsibility. You are responsible for making the contributions that will move you forward. You have to move from standing on the sidelines to becoming an active participant in building your own momentum. Remember, you are the architect who is designing moments that will propel you forward toward reaching your big goals. The very essence of Moment Momentum is using every moment as an opportunity to turn potential energy into the kinetic action that builds unstoppable momentum.

Accountability: The Foundation of Ownership

If you truly want to convert your thoughts into action, you must take accountability for your efforts. You must understand your role and how your contributions impact each moment. Developing accountability demands a consistent effort and lots of self-reflection. Or as we would say in New England, "Cowboy up and own your sh*t." How ya like them apples?

For many, the accountability muscle is weak. The more chaotic life becomes, the easier it is for excuses to snowball. It works like this: Getting up late means not making yourself a healthy lunch, so you grab a burger and fries for lunch at a local burger joint near work. Since you already "ruined" your chance to eat healthy today, you decide to have pizza for dinner. All that heavy food puts you in a food coma once you get home, which stops you from going to the gym. So, instead, you decide to pull up Netflix and watch a movie. Who watches a movie without popcorn? Before you know it, you're elbow-deep in a bucket of Orville Redenbacher. You end the night with a "small" bowl of ice cream to reward yourself for a hard day.

Excuses: 6. Accountability: 0.

You are not alone. We all need to strengthen our accountability muscles. Here are some key strategies to "own your sh*t":

- **Be real with yourself:** Regularly take a look at your actions and their consequences. You can be honest without being harsh. Give yourself the valuable feedback you need to change bad patterns of behavior, identify where you need to grow, and stay on the path of creating momentum.

- **Get comfortable with discomfort:** Taking accountability means you are going to have to confront some uncomfortable truths about yourself. You will need to own your mistakes, admit where you are falling short, and face the consequences of your actions. I'm not going to lie—this can suck big time. But it's necessary to grow. How badly do you want to build momentum? Your willingness to get uncomfortable will give you the answer.

- **Be solution focused:** It's too easy to get caught up dwelling on past mistakes. You need to focus on finding solutions to move forward. Identify small steps you can take to move you in the right direction. Momentum can be built with even tiny steps.

- **Seek "valuable" feedback:** Feedback is crucial for making adjustments and moving forward. But you need to seek that feedback from "valuable" sources—that is, the people you trust, love, and respect. They know you well enough to identify your blind spots and give relevant insights to help you be more accountable.

- **Track your progress:** Keep a journal where you can track your progress. Write down your successes and failures. Celebrate when you succeed, and forgive yourself when you fail. Two steps forward and one step back is still progress. But you need to track your steps so you know where you are.

- **Be kind to yourself:** Owning your sh*t doesn't mean you need to beat yourself up all the time. You have learned how to dance that tango with failure and forgiveness, so put your dancing shoes on, turn up the music, and forgive yourself when you step on your own toes.
- **Focus on your circle of influence:** You might not be able to control everything that happens in your life, but you can control how you respond. Focus on the things you can control: your attitude, the choices you make, and the actions you take. When you do, you empower yourself to create the change you need to build momentum for yourself and others.

Accountability is a journey, not a destination. You will have good days and bad days of holding yourself accountable. Learn to celebrate the good days and push through the bad. The goal is growth and forward progress, not perfection.

Take a Moment

The Accountability Audit

Take a few minutes to reflect on a recent moment you wished you could get back. Ask yourself: How did I react in the moment? What were the consequences of my actions? What role did I play in creating the outcome? What could I have done differently? What did I learn from this experience?

An Accountability Intervention

Jim Trick is the co-owner of Marblehead Opticians, an accomplished singer/songwriter, a Brazilian jujitsu instructor, and the host of the popular podcast *My White Belt*. He is a force of nature and has been one of my best friends for the past 20 years. Jim is currently working on his memoir, *Morbidly*, which outlines his extraordinary battle with weight management. Having struggled with his weight for most of his life, the magnitude of his issue became clear on a sunny afternoon in 1991.

As he tells it:

> My friends were off with their girlfriends or at work, and I was sitting alone in the parking lot of a Kentucky Fried Chicken. I was about to engage in my first hardcore binge. It was a family meal, with eight pieces of fried chicken with sides of mashed potatoes and biscuits. I didn't feel sick, throw up, or feel any pain. I wish I had. I wish it hadn't tasted good, felt good, or provided comfort, but it did. It became normal, but as legendary singer/songwriter Bruce Cockburn once said, "The trouble with normal is that it only gets worse."

Eight years later, a "normal" day of eating for Jim had ballooned out of control, often topping more than 5,000 calories. His struggles culminated in a moment of harsh reality. Jim continued:

> I remember one night I came home to find my electricity had been turned off. My financial life was as out of control as my eating. I had been out with friends and decided to end the day alone with a large pizza. There I sat, eating my pizza by flashlight before calling to have the power turned back on. I had become morbidly obese. At 430 pounds, with a 66-inch waist, I could not pee standing up, sit in a restaurant booth, buy clothes in a normal store, walk without my knees killing me, or fly in a plane without buying two seats. I was desperate, and you know what desperate times require.

Jim's desperate measure was to undergo gastric bypass surgery. In the months that followed the surgery, the pounds melted away as if by magic. Losing more than 200 pounds, Jim enjoyed life as a "thin man" for nearly two years. He was told by his doctors that the bypass was a tool, not a cure. While Jim nodded in agreement, he eventually ignored their orders. Jim fell back into his old habits. While his accountability faded away, the weight came back with a vengeance. Before he knew it, Jim was morbidly obese once again.

It wasn't until a few friends staged a loving intervention with Jim that he realized his eating was out of control. He decided to hold himself accountable and own his moment. He needed a new approach—one that wasn't a "silver bullet" but a total lifestyle overhaul. He began to meal prep and make better choices with his food. He started to go on daily walks. He enrolled in a beginner's class at a local Brazilian jujitsu studio and attended their classes several nights a week. He was kind to himself, practicing forgiveness when he made the occasional "bad" choice.

Fast-forward 10 years, and Jim has once again lost more than 200 pounds and continues to maintain his healthy lifestyle. Accountability has no shortcuts. It requires daily choices, sometimes moment by moment.

Overcoming Accountability Obstacles

As I have said before, accountability is a journey. Along that journey will be challenges, setbacks, and unexpected detours. These obstacles can feel incredibly daunting, threatening to derail your progress. However, it's in these moments of adversity that your commitment to ownership is tested and strengthened. Facing these obstacles head-on is how you build resilience, resourcefulness, and perseverance.

Let's face it: obstacles are inevitable and sometimes unavoidable. They are part of the overarching human experience. Obstacles can take many different forms—from personal challenges like illness or loss to professional setbacks like losing your job to relational challenges like conflict or misunderstandings. It can be so tempting to just give up, relinquish your ownership rights, and play a victim of circumstance. But these are the moments when you need to double down on your commitment.

Overcoming obstacles is a skill you can develop through deliberate intention and conscious practice. Here are some effective strategies you can use to face your obstacles:

- **Reframe your perspective:** When you find yourself facing an obstacle, try not to jump immediately to an inevitable catastrophic end. Instead, reframe the challenge as an opportunity to find new solutions. Use your WITWAW approach to bring a sense of optimism and find a way to build momentum.
- **Use Moment Momentum:** Don't get overwhelmed by a massive obstacle. Think through how you can use individual moments to work around the obstacle. Breaking down the strategy to overcome the obstacle into small moments makes it more accessible and encourages accountability. The challenge becomes far less daunting and spreads ownership to a group of people. Remember, momentum is a team sport.
- **Focus on your strengths:** Think back to when you faced other obstacles and remind yourself of your past successes. Ask yourself, "What strengths helped me overcome challenges in the past and how can I use them in this current situation?" This exercise can boost your confidence and build your resilience.
- **Learn to fail forward:** Not every moment is going to be successful. You need to break down failures into learning

moments and avoid repeating the same mistakes. If you learn from each mistake, you better the odds of succeeding in the future.

- **Remember your purpose:** Setbacks can require a deeper sense of meaning to overcome. Remind yourself why overcoming this obstacle is important to you. What are you doing this for? Who are you doing this for? Reconnect with your purpose and rekindle the motivation you need to rebuild momentum.

It's Not About Your Talent

Taking accountability and owning your actions in a moment can dramatically differentiate between seizing the opportunities you desire and missing out on them. When coaching clients, I often emphasize that while talent is valuable, it is hard work and the willingness to tackle tasks that you might not want to do that truly set you apart. This mindset cultivates a discipline that can propel you ahead of the competition.

Many people fall into the trap of allowing obstacles to stop them or waiting for the perfect moment or the "right" task to come along, believing that their moment of success is just around the corner. However, this passive approach can lead to missed opportunities. Instead, those who actively take responsibility—those who do the unglamorous, tedious, or challenging work—often find themselves in the right place at the right time. This proactive ownership is crucial because it demonstrates reliability, builds trust, and ultimately opens doors to opportunities that might otherwise remain closed.

Are you willing to tackle moments you don't want to? Your answer will have a profound effect on your success. If you commit yourself to doing one thing a day that you don't want to do, you will find yourself slowly edging out the competition and building the momentum to achieve your big goal.

> **Take a Moment**
>
> **The Obstacle Analysis**
>
> Identify a current obstacle you are facing. How can you reframe your perspective on it? What are three small steps you can take to rebuild momentum? Remind yourself why overcoming this obstacle is important to you.

Real-World Application: Hurricane Helene

On September 27, 2024, most of the country watched in horror as Hurricane Helene devastated western North Carolina. It left catastrophic damage in towns like Asheville and the surrounding communities, compiling a death toll of more than 230 people. Hundreds of roads and bridges were simply washed away. Residents were stranded on different mountains, needing to be airlifted to safety. Seeing the enormity of the obstacles these towns face, it is easy to understand the overwhelming darkness surrounding the situation. But as more inspiring words from Bruce Cockburn remind us, "Nothing worth having comes without some kind of fight; got to kick at the darkness 'til it bleeds daylight."

My undying commitment to hope makes me believe that the good people of North Carolina have the resilience to rebuild and own this moment. The framework to overcome obstacles outlined earlier can be used to do the following:

- **Reframe their perspective:** They will need to ask, "What if there was a way?" more than they ever have before. What if there was a way to rebuild the roads to lessen traffic? What if there was a way to support local business owners cut off from their customers? What if there was a way to design bridges to withstand flash flooding? Although this wasn't asked for, this is an opportunity for improvement.

- **Use Moment Momentum:** The overall devastation is too much to tackle as a whole. There will need to be a plan to break down actions into moments that everyone can own. The locals, the volunteers, the state, and the federal government will all need to build momentum off small achievable moments that create a sense of belonging, understanding, meaning, and purpose.

- **Focus on their strengths:** There will need to be a division of strengths. Placing people in roles that they can excel in will not only speed up the process but produce better results. When it's all-hands-on-deck, skills are sometimes pushed aside for the need of "warm bodies" to simply help with the large amount of work to be done. Keeping everyone in their respective lanes may feel like it is slowing down the process, but as the Navy Seals will tell you, "Slow is smooth, and smooth is fast."

- **Learn to fail forward:** It is completely understandable to be overwhelmed by the damage. As hard as it is to look at it, everyone will need to learn from "why" things happened. Why did certain things fail? Why aren't current strategies working? These are difficult questions to ask, but the valuable insights the answers will provide make it worth the uncomfortableness.

- **Remember their purpose:** North Carolina has a deep, rich history of taking actions of true character rather than self-serving displays. That is the impetus of their state motto, *Esse Quam Videri*, which translates as "To be rather than to seem." Rebuilding is going to require a deep, authentic connection to generations of families and where they call home. There will be days when rebuilding will feel impossible, but North Carolina can and will be rebuilt, one moment at a time.

The Ripple Effect of Ownership

Have you ever been on a team where everyone just sits around staring at each other, waiting for "the boss" to take the lead? The apathy is palpable, and momentum is destroyed. Contrast that with a collaborative group where everyone feels a sense of ownership. The ideas flow like Niagara Falls, challenges are met head-on, everyone owns their moments, unstoppable momentum is built, and the big goal is achieved. That's the power of ownership.

When you own your moments, you create a profound impact. You're not just responsible for completing a task; you're now invested in a moment's success. You create a ripple effect that spreads out in four distinct directions. Your investment now influences not just your own performance but also team dynamics, the organizational culture, and ultimately society as a whole.

The Personal Ripple

When you own your moments, the most immediate impact you feel is in your own performance. You switch from simply going through the motions to being actively engaged in the outcome. Owning your moments creates an intrinsic motivation that drives creativity, amps up performance, and elevates the overall quality of your work. You stop being reactive, and instead, you proactively anticipate potential challenges, taking the initiative to plan possible solutions before they are needed. You bounce back from setbacks quickly and with more resilience. You end up giving your personal development journey significant momentum.

Owning your moments fosters real accountability. You develop more self-awareness and become more likely to pursue opportunities to improve your skills. You realize that asking for help is not showing weakness; it's showing your commitment to overall success. Your commitment to continuous improvement ends up building your competence and confidence, which strengthens your willingness to own your moments.

The Team Ripple

Owning your moments isn't just about personal gain. It also influences interactions with your team. When others see you hold yourself accountable, you are perceived as more reliable and trustworthy. Your teammates won't fear working with you because they know you will do your part. This strengthens the team dynamic, deepens your connections, and creates a more collaborative environment.

Ownership earns you respect. When the entire team takes ownership, they create a sense of belonging, bring clarity to understanding, increase a sense of meaning, and unite all team members for a greater purpose. Team ownership makes BUMP-ing a moment much easier and more effective. Taking ownership brings unique contributions to the surface and allows for more innovation and best practices to be cultivated, benefiting the entire team.

The Organizational Ripple

The ripple effect of owning your moments can extend through the entire organization. When you influence your teammates to own their moments, you can end up changing the entire culture of the company. Your accountability inspires others to take the initiative, make decisions, and own their role in building momentum, improving overall efficiency, and speeding up the timeline to achieving the big goal.

Influencing others to take ownership can also lead to better retention and employee engagement for the organization. When employees feel a sense of ownership, they feel seen, heard, and valued as an integral part of the company's success. They create a culture that people want to be a part of, aiding in the recruitment of better-qualified candidates and further contributing to the long-term success of the organization.

The Societal Ripple

When you commit to owning your moments, the ripple effect you create washes into your personal life. You end up taking ownership of your life, influencing your family, your community, and society as a whole. You become an active participant in every aspect of your life. From the dinner table to the PTA meeting to the kid's soccer team to the local soup kitchen, you actively begin to shape the world around you, contributing to the betterment of society.

Ownership is more than a mindset; it's a movement. It's the path to a more vibrant, productive, harmonious world. So own your moments. Take responsibility for your actions. Invest in your personal growth and contribute to a better world.

Take a Moment

Your Team Impact

Think about a time when your ownership influenced your team. Describe how your accountability affected team dynamics and collaboration. Did it lead to a more trusting and reliable environment? How did it contribute to the team's overall success?

Moments to Remember:

- Ownership is the bridge between dreaming and doing.
- Ownership isn't about taking control; it's about taking responsibility.
- Accountability is a journey, not a destination. You will have good days and bad days of holding yourself accountable.
- Obstacles are inevitable and sometimes unavoidable.
- The ripple effect of owning your moment influences yourself, your team, your organization, and ultimately society as a whole.

14

Track the KPI of Hope: Managing Your Desires and Expectations

Momentum Objectives:

- Understand the KPI of hope.
- Analyze the role of desires and expectations.
- Implement strategies for aligning desires with actions.
- Explore the alchemy of hope.
- Embrace the power of the unexpected.
- Learn to track and measure hope.

WHENEVER I MENTION the word *hope* to my CEO clients, they always get this enigmatic look on their faces as they internally ask themselves what the key performance indicator (KPI) of Hope is. They often treat *hope* as a four-letter word they have no interest in hearing. But when it comes to achieving big goals and building unstoppable momentum, hope is much more than just a feel-good emotion. It actually *is* a KPI of sorts that can be actively cultivated, tracked, and managed (every ear in the C-suite just perked up). Just as your CFO takes those financial KPI spreadsheets home at night to look at them like a sexy *Bloomberg Businessweek* center-fold, you should also take a look at your KPI of Hope for valuable insights into your motivation and overall happiness.

Taking a look at your KPI of Hope isn't about crossing your fingers and waiting to see what destiny is willing to fork over. And there is no magic lamp to rub that will produce hope in a puff of smoke. This is about the tangible role that hope plays in building momentum. Hope can be broken down into two simple things: *desires* and *expectations*. Your motivation gets its oomph from your desires, and your path gets its guidance from your expectations. If you can align your desires and expectations, you can generate an overflowing well of hope.

When desires and expectations become misaligned, you will find yourself facing varying levels of hopelessness. Having unrealistic expectations leads to feelings of frustration at best and the desire to quit at worst. If you mismanage your desires, you will become increasingly impatient and even more discouraged.

Imagine you have been angling for that promotion you desperately want. If you expect the promotion to come as a result of what you've already been doing—without really ramping up your effort in a way that's impactful and measurable—then you're setting yourself up to feel disappointed when the promotion doesn't happen. If you can find that sweet spot where your ambition meets the realistic expectations of your effort, you can capture hope long enough to build momentum and reach your goals.

Understanding Your Desires

Understanding what you truly want and why you want it can shed light on the path you should choose to reach your goals. If you want to be filled with hope when designing moments of momentum, you have to figure out in what direction you want to go.

Your desires act as the compass of your moments. They will guide you to a future aligned with what matters most to you.

Unmasking the Truth

For some people, unmasking true desires can feel like a highly vulnerable act of selfishness. The influence of suffocating layers of societal, family, and personal expectations can make you believe you want something that you actually don't. If you want to be able to live a hope-filled life, you will have to find time for introspection, some bone-crushing honesty, and a willingness to accept your truth.

Here are some helpful ways to figure out what you truly want:

- **Explore Your Mariana Trench:** Discovering what you really desire is not a surface activity. It requires diving into the deepest part of your soul, your personal Mariana Trench (the deepest part of the ocean), to find what your heart is focused on. This may take some repeated questions of "Why?" to get below the surface. Keep asking yourself why you desire something until you've reached the ultimate truth.
- **Question your beliefs:** Have you ever challenged why you believe something is a desire of yours? Is the desire rooted in your non-negotiable values? Is it something you inherited from someone else? Are your desires serving you in a positive way, or are they actually holding you back? Don't just blindly accept your reasons as gospel. Remember your brain craves certainty ... not necessarily truth.
- **Expose your emotions:** Getting to the truth requires some serious vulnerability. The truth often arrives with powerful emotions attached to it. Don't be afraid of exposing your emotions to yourself. Bringing your emotions to the surface can help in healing past wounds and serve as proof that what you think is the truth actually is the truth.

Take a Moment

Tell Me Whatcha Want, Whatcha Really, Really Want

Write down one of your deepest desires. Challenge your desire as if you didn't believe it. Is your desire rooted in your values? Which ones and why? Is this desire serving you well? How so? Don't let yourself off the hook too easily. Be able to defend your answers with specific reasons.

"Frankensteining" Your Desires

Once you've discovered your true desires, you need to bring them to life like Dr. Frankenstein did. Your desires need to be acknowledged and energized so they can be factored into your decision-making, goal-setting, and momentum-building.

Here are some ways to pull that lightning switch:

- **Put pen to paper:** If you don't write down your desires, are they even real? You need to convert your ambition into reality and put pen to paper. This action can help clarify your desires and make them a real living thing.
- **Create an alternate reality:** Visualizing what your life will look like when your desires are fulfilled can be a powerful motivator. Professional athletes use this technique to visualize that putt going in, that homerun being hit, or that touchdown being made. Visualizing will help connect your desires to the emotions you can use to motivate yourself to build momentum.
- **Speak it until you believe it:** Repeating positive affirmations to yourself that reflect your desires can reprogram your brain and align your thoughts with actions. Remember, what the eyes see and the ears hear, the mind believes.

Aligning Your Desires with Your Actions

Getting to the bottom of your desires is only the first step in managing your hope. The next step is aligning your desires with some real action. This requires serious deliberate intention to ensure you stay disciplined to make choices that align with your deepest yearnings.

Here are some suggestions to help you align your desires with real action:

- **Put your desires first:** This might seem selfish on the surface, but putting your desires first helps you align your actions with your goal. Saying "no" to things that pull you away from your desires will help keep you on the right path and help conserve your energy for the actions that will move you forward.
- **Convert your desires to goals:** Saying you want something isn't the same as accomplishing it. You need to transform your desires into measurable goals, which will allow you to create a clear plan to design the moments that will get you where you want to go.
- **Track where you are at:** Monitor your progress as much as possible. Monitoring progress will allow you to celebrate small wins along the way, learn from your setbacks, and pivot when you need to, enabling you all the while to maintain the momentum you build.

It's important to understand that desires can and will change. The more life you live, the more clarity you gain as to what you want out of it. Treating your desires as dynamic choices that evolve will enable you to adjust your course and sustain momentum.

The Alchemy of Hope: Balancing Your Desires and Expectations

Our hope is built by the twin engines of desire and expectation. Desire is what we want to happen; it is the ideal scenario we envision. Expectation, on the other hand, is what we believe is going to happen; it is our forecast of the future based on evidence of the past and the current circumstances at hand. When these two forces are aligned, we generate the hope we need to build momentum. But when they are misaligned, the hopelessness that occurs can derail our moments and stop all forward progress.

Desire Is the Seed of Hope

Hope sprouts from the fertile ground of your desires. When you empower yourself to fully embrace what you truly desire, you end up watering that seed of hope, giving it the ability to blossom into something extraordinary. When your desires and hopes begin to mingle, they shape what your future could look like.

Every moment that you aren't focused on your desires can feel like a betrayal of your hope. This feeling of unfaithfulness arises because your desires are deeply connected to your sense of self. They represent what you think you are capable of. When you ignore your desires, it can feel like you are giving up on your dreams.

WARNING: It is incredibly important to distinguish between "healthy" desires that inspire and motivate you and "unhealthy" desires that can lead to suffering and devastation. Healthy desires align with your non-negotiable values and aim to fulfill your purpose. They are the root of hope. Unhealthy desires are rooted in fear and the need for external validation. They grow into future obstacles that will stop your momentum.

The goal is to cultivate desires that are born from the things that matter most to you. Achieving these desires will make you a better version of yourself and amplify true and lasting hope.

Expectation Is the Lens of Hope

Expectations are simply predictions of an uncertain future. They act as the lens through which you view your desires, based on past experiences, current circumstances, and perceived possibilities. Expectations influence your perception, emotions, reactions, and exactly how much hope you feel.

When you have realistic expectations, the opportunity for hope is found in every twist and turn. When your expectations are based on current reality, you are able to adapt to the potentially dangerous road ahead by keeping an accurate sense of perspective. You become empowered to quickly change lanes and find the best route toward your desires. Even when the journey gets difficult and unforeseen obstacles appear in your path, realistic expectations can generate the hope you need to find resilience and stay on track.

When your expectations are unrealistic, they set you up for disappointment and inevitably kick hope in the nether regions. Whether overly optimistic or too pessimistic, unrealistic expectations create a fragile foundation for hope. Over time, repeated disappointments can diminish your capacity for hope and darken your view of the future.

Take a Moment

Balancing Hope

Write down one of your current desires. What do you realistically expect to happen regarding your desire? Take a minute to analyze whether your expectation is overly optimistic, overly pessimistic, or reasonable considering the circumstances. Make adjustments as necessary.

The Power of the Unexpected

When your expectations are destroyed, it can be an unsettling experience. The 2024 U.S. presidential election serves as a prime example of this phenomenon, where nearly half the country would find their hopes and beliefs shattered. As divided as the United States is at the moment, it can be difficult to find hope no matter which side of the aisle you are on.

However, it is important to recognize that beneath the seemingly monumental differences and emotionally charged debates, the fundamental desires and aspirations of the American people are remarkably similar. Most Americans want a better future for themselves and their loved ones, a stable economy, access to quality healthcare and education, and a sense of security and belonging. It's in the "how" those desires are met where things get off-track. This is where emotions step in and often ruin any opportunity to find common ground.

In times of shattered expectations, one of the most effective ways to restore your hope is through the power of the unexpected. When you encounter something that challenges your preconceived notions or defies your assumptions, it can open your mind to different perspectives.

Here are some ways you can do something unexpected for someone to help repair broken expectations:

- **Perform a random act of kindness:** Random acts of kindness have the remarkable ability to transcend political and ideological boundaries. A kind word, gesture, or deed can create a moment of genuine human connection, which is a powerful antidote to the hostility so common in today's divided society. These acts of kindness can take many forms and are limited only by your imagination and willingness to seize an opportunity to make someone's day a little brighter.

Buy that coffee for the car behind you in the drive-thru, hold that door open, or stop and help change a stranger's tire. You never know how much any of these might mean to the recipient or how far the effect can ripple.

- **Collaborate with an "opponent":** Working closely with someone you might ordinarily consider an "opponent" can be an eye-opening experience. It forces you to confront and reconsider your preconceived notions and emotional biases. Consider joining forces on a community project with someone whose ideologies differ from yours. Whether it's organizing a neighborhood cleanup, volunteering at a local shelter, or working together on a school board initiative, these collaborations can foster mutual respect and understanding and shift your expectations.
- **Share a powerful story of restored expectations:** Stories have the unique ability to change hearts and minds, especially when they highlight personal journeys of overcoming shattered expectations. Sharing a story about a time when your assumptions were challenged and ultimately transformed can inspire others to reevaluate their own perspectives. Whether you recount a story to a friend or co-worker, or post on a social media platform, these stories can foster a more inclusive and empathetic society.

These unexpected experiences serve as reminders that, despite our differences, we are all human beings with the capacity for empathy, understanding, and collaboration.

A Random Act of Kindness on Mt. Everest

On a recent episode of my podcast, *Just a Moment*, I was able to interview my dear friend and legendary American polar explorer and mountaineer Alison Levine. Alison is one of only 20 people on the planet who have completed the Adventure Grand Slam.

She has climbed the seven highest peaks in the world and crossed both the North and South Poles. What makes her accomplishments even more incredible is that the 5'4", 100-pound dynamo was born with a hole in her heart and has had three surgeries to repair it.

Alison experienced the ultimate random act of kindness during her second attempt at summiting Mount Everest. As she tells it:

The most challenging climb I ever had was, of course, Mount Everest. And I've been to that mountain twice. The first in 2002 as the team captain for the first American women's Mount Everest expedition, and I had never turned back from a summit, from a big summit until that climb. And during that expedition in 2002, our team got caught in bad weather at 28,750 feet above sea level.

Far up into the Death Zone, just a couple hundred feet from the summit of Mount Everest. And we had to turn back because of bad weather. That was a gut-wrenching decision because you're on that mountain for two months. We had scrounged for sponsorship funding, and the Ford Motor Company had stepped up and sponsored us.

We had trained, we were on the mountain, we had tons of media coverage because we were the first American women's Everest expedition. We had hundreds of media outlets following our climb from all over the world. And then we didn't make it. So to have such a high-profile failure, everybody's talking about the fact that you didn't make it.

We did all this media before we left for the mountain. And then after our failed attempt, we had to come back, go to all the same TV shows, again, talk to all the media outlets again, and just talk about this failure over and over and over. And it's hard to have a public failure like that, especially to be the butt of Jay Leno's opening monologue joke made me so self-conscious.

While Alison had all the motivation necessary to reach the summit, her ability to do so was severely affected by the incoming storm, resulting in a heart-breaking failure. That failure had a massive influence on her expectations and desire to try again.

Feeling like I let everybody down ... because we really wanted to achieve this incredible goal and we didn't do it. And I very much internalized that failure for a long time.

A long time turned into eight years of building up the confidence to try to summit Mount Everest again. After weeks of climbing, Alison found herself once again at 28,750 feet. And that is where she experienced a moment that changed everything.

There is a situation I had on my second Everest attempt. I'm at the South Summit again. The South Summit is where I turned around in 2002. I'm approaching the South Summit again. Weather comes in. Clouds come in. It's dumping snow. Teams were turning back and calling it quits. And I'm thinking, how is it possible? I am back here in the same exact situation, trying to go for the summit ... and in comes a storm.

Little did Alison know that legendary mountain guide Michael Horst was waiting for her. He knew Alison's story and that the South Summit was where she turned around eight years prior. He was about to perform an act of kindness that would change Alison forever.

I hear this voice saying, "Alison! Hey Alison!" Somebody's calling me. I'm thinking I'm hallucinating. I'm hearing things. You know, your brain is so oxygen-starved that it's not unusual for people to hallucinate at that elevation. I must be hearing things. The voice gets louder. "Alison! Alison!" I'm thinking, what the hell?

I see it's this guide, Michael Horst. I said, Michael ... WHAT?! What do you want? And I'm super annoyed. This guy is distracting me.

I am on this summit ridge that is an 8,000-foot drop on one side, a 10,000-foot drop on the other. And some guy is trying to get my attention to talk to me. What? What do you want?

He said, "I need you to make me a promise. I need you to promise me that you're going to go farther than this."

He anticipated that I might be feeling some anxiety about going farther in that storm and those few words of encouragement ...

He said, "You promise me." We shook on the promise. Like I said, I never break a promise. That encouragement just gave me so much more energy and so much more confidence, and I have never forgotten that.

And that's why I say a few kind words of encouragement shared with somebody who is having some doubts can completely change the outcome of a situation. That's what changes the world.

Alison experienced one of the most powerful acts of kindness I have ever heard of. Powerful enough to push her to the summit of Mt. Everest. Alison has made it her mission to reach out to those in need of support and give them the encouragement they need to reset their expectations.

Take a Moment

The Levine Lift

Identify someone in your life who could use a little encouragement. Reach out to them and offer a few words of support related to a goal they are pursuing. Be specific and genuine in your encouragement. Reflect on how this act of kindness makes you feel and how it might alter the expectations of the other person.

A Difficult Balancing Act

Finding the sweet spot to balance desires and expectations is not easy. It requires constant nudging and recalibrating. But finding this balance is the key to sustainable hope. Here are some strategies for trying to balance the two:

- **Practice acceptance:** Learn to accept what is in your control and let go of what isn't. The more you can surrender to this reality, the more mental energy you free up to be used elsewhere.
- **Focus on the process:** Don't get hyperfocused on the end goal. Placing too much emphasis on achieving the big goal can overwhelm you, steal your hope, and stop momentum.
- **Detach yourself:** Try not to get overly attached to a specific outcome. Recognize there are many roads to your destination, and all of them will get you there eventually. This detachment will help prevent disappointment when one path doesn't take you where you want to go.
- **Inspire yourself:** Seek out inspiration wherever you can. Watch that inspiring video, speak to that mentor, take a walk in nature, pet your dog—whatever it takes to feed your soul with something positive.
- **Serve others:** Taking the focus off yourself and placing it on helping someone in need is a great way to rejuvenate your belief in humankind and balance the scales of desire and expectations.

It's important to understand that this balancing act is a hands-on process. This is not a one-time action that will forever balance your desires and expectations. It's like standing on those scales at the doctor's office, staring at the dreaded slider as the nurse nudges the weight back and forth until the realization of the truth is exposed—no matter how painful the truth might be.

Tracking the KPI of Hope: Measuring What Matters

While most CEOs perceive hope as intangible, they would be wrong. Hope can, in fact, be measured and managed. Just as most organizations track KPIs to gauge progress toward their established goals, you can track your KPI of Hope to get a better understanding of your state of mind and identify areas of potential improvement.

To track your progress, you will need to establish some defined metrics that reflect your level of hope and identify whether your hope is growing or diminishing. This assessment is about capturing valuable data that you can use to balance your desires and expectations and sustain a level of hope that builds resilience and momentum.

Defining Your Hope Metrics

The first step in tracking your KPI of Hope is to define the metrics that can be measured. These are the areas in your life that are most affected by hope, and they will vary from person to person. Here are some common examples:

- **Your mood:** How often do you feel excited and hopeful? How often do you feel disheartened and hopeless?
- **Your motivation:** How driven are you to pursue your desires? Do you feel a sense of purpose and meaning, or do you feel lost and uninterested?
- **Your resilience:** Do you bounce back quickly from setbacks? Do challenges diminish your hope?
- **Your belief in yourself:** How confident are you in your ability to achieve your desires? Do you have the skills necessary for success?
- **Your engagement:** How actively are you pursuing your goals? Are you seeking out new experiences, or are you withdrawing and feeling disconnected?

- **Your physical well-being:** How is your physical health? Are you stressed out? Are you feeling a heavy sense of anxiety? Are you tired?
- **Your connections:** How strong are your personal connections? Do you feel supported in pursuing your desires?

Take a Moment

Convert to the Metric System

Choose three metrics of hope that resonate with you. What do these metrics reveal about your current level of hope? What can you do to increase these metrics individually?

Developing Your Tracking System

Once you have identified your hope metrics, develop a simple system for tracking them. It is only by tracking them that you can analyze where you are finding success with regard to your level of hope and where you should be investing your efforts. Here are some of the different ways you can track your hope metrics:

- **Keeping a journal:** Writing down your thoughts and feelings related to your hope metrics is a great way to track where you are at. Being able to look at specific entries can provide valuable insight into your emotional state of mind and help you identify trends.
- **Using mood tracking apps:** Mood tracking apps like Daylio and EMoods can monitor your emotions throughout the day and over a long period of time. Using these can help identify triggers that influence your mood.
- **Making a self-assessment spreadsheet:** Where my spreadsheet peeps at?! Create an Excel spreadsheet of your metrics that allows you to track everything. Devise a numbers

system for your metrics that will allow you to total them. Find the over/under on when you have hope and when you don't. Is anyone else getting excited?!

- **Using physical health monitoring apps:** Track your health with apps like MyFitnessPal or Fitbit to monitor your progress. Look at your sleep patterns, number of workouts, and the food you are eating. Address any imbalances to feel better and raise your level of hope.

No matter how you decide to track things, you will need to routinely look at the data you collect to identify relevant trends and patterns. Digging into everything from the time of day to the days of the week can reveal important information about when you feel hopeful. Analyzing the data will help you find the triggers to avoid and the triggers to lean into for the best results.

Taking Action

Based on what your analysis of the data reveals, you may need to rebalance your desires and expectations. Remember, this process is dynamic, not static. More than likely, as your current circumstances fluctuate, so will your approach. To rebalance and sustain your hope, you may need to do the following:

- **Revisit your desires:** Are your desires still in alignment with your values? Are you feeling a sense of purpose when pursuing your desires? Making some adjustments might be necessary in order to stay inspired and motivated.
- **Recalibrate your expectations:** Making sure your expectations are realistic is incredibly important to maintaining hope. Have your circumstances changed? Do you need to tweak your expectations with the new information available? Make the adjustments to avoid any unnecessary disappointments.

At its core, hope is about resistance and resilience. Life can take a turn for the worse in a heartbeat; a single moment can engulf your future in darkness. Occasionally, the weight of the present moment can crush you. The very air you are breathing can be heavy with grief and disappointment. In these moments of profound darkness, all it takes is a whisper of despair to make you believe that the light will never return.

But hope, that persistent spark, can be a stubborn son-of-a-b*tch when trying to be extinguished. If you can keep your eyes focused on your desires and make the necessary adjustments to your expectations, your flame and future will both be safe.

Moments to Remember:
- Hope is a combination of desires and expectations.
- When desires and expectations become misaligned, you will find yourself facing varying levels of hopelessness.
- The influence of suffocating layers of societal, family, and personal expectations can make you believe you desire something that you actually don't.
- Desires need to be acknowledged and energized to be factored into your decision-making, goal-setting, and momentum-building.
- Treating your desires as dynamic choices that evolve and change will enable you to adjust your course and sustain momentum.
- Desire is the seed of hope; expectation is the lens of hope.
- In times of shattered expectations, one of the most effective ways to restore your hope is through the power of the unexpected.
- Finding the sweet spot to balance desires and expectations is not easy. It requires constant nudging and recalibrating. But finding this balance is the key to sustainable hope.
- Hope can be managed through defined metrics.

15

Build a Moment-Driven Legacy: Designing a Life Worth Remembering

Momentum Objectives:

- Understand the "2nd Life" effort.
- Use concentric circles of influence to build momentum.
- Maximize inner circle impact.
- Expand your influence indirectly.
- Build systemic impact.
- Produce cumulative impact.

IN THE YEAR following my son Theo's death, I spiraled into a deep depression. I slowly pulled away from almost everything and sentenced myself to a self-imposed banishment from the idea of happiness. I stayed busy to keep my mind occupied, but my life had stopped gaining momentum. Having his death happen during the pandemic made it incredibly hard to mourn. The strict gathering policies made inviting those who wanted to say

their goodbyes properly impossible. There would be no celebration of his life. So how could I possibly celebrate anything in mine?

Eighteen months had passed when I received a phone call from a
dear friend who was deeply concerned about my well-being. I was
mostly disengaged during the conversation and just wanted to
hang up and get on with my day. He got quiet for a moment and
then said to me, "I understand you have been through something
horrific. I hate that you had to go through it. But I want you to
know something truly important. I believe when you die, you
really die twice. The first time is when you leave this earth, but
the second is when your name is spoken for the last time. So
what I want to know is what are you doing to make sure Theo's
second life outlives his first? Because this wallowing won't
get it done."

Ugh, I'm getting choked up as I try to type this. Talk about an
OGRE moment. The guts it took to have that conversation with
me was astronomical. His words stung. It felt like a 240-pound
hockey defenseman just checked me into the boards. I tried to
respond, but the power of his words knocked the breath out of
me. After the awkward silence, I told him he was right. He
BUMPed me forward and broke that freeze response to stress
I had been living in since Theo passed. He had established that
sense of belonging by walking through the grieving process with
me for more than a year; he clearly understood how I was feeling
and injected incredible meaning into his intervention with me.
He questioned my purpose, knowing that I had an insatiable
desire to help others, and he challenged me to live it.

I slowly started to pull myself out of the depression by focusing
only on the moment I was currently facing. I knew I could manage that. I did everything I could to build momentum one moment
at a time. My life began to shift. I had to face some harsh realities
and make some incredibly difficult decisions. It hurt. A lot. But
I knew I had to make them to continue building momentum.

So here we are. In my best Joey Tribbiani (from the *Friends* TV show) voice ... "How you doin?" I can't begin to explain to you how much I want to see you succeed and begin to craft an unforgettable legacy of hope and positive impact. It's totally possible. But it's going to take work. It's going to take what I now call *2nd Life* effort. This is about making such a powerful impact that people talk about you for generations after you are gone. I believe the length of your 2nd Life is directly correlated to how much momentum you created for others. So let's take a look at how to do that.

Using Concentric Circles of Influence

I first heard the phrase *concentric circles* when speaking to our booking agent back in my touring days with Big Kettle Drum. The agent was talking about the band Sister Hazel and how they grew from a local college bar band in Gainesville, Florida, to a national act that sells out almost every venue they play. Sister Hazel didn't run all over the country, playing wherever they could get a gig. That would be crazy (and exactly what we were doing). He said they worked in concentric circles, playing three cities within a six hour radius, rotating through them every four to six weeks to stay top-of-mind and build an audience. It made sense. They started closest to home, went out a little further, and then a little further again before coming back to home base. This strategy helped them maximize their influence until it reached across the country.

Using moments to build legacy works the same. Your innermost circle (closest to home) represents those you have direct influence over and interactions with. The next circle represents the indirect influence you have. This is the occasional interaction, with people and co-workers you don't interact with every day, through your networks and relationships. The outermost circle represents systemic influence. This is the impact you have on the world at large through your contributions and participation in larger systems.

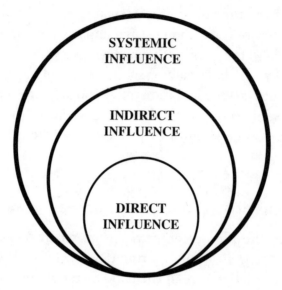

Maximizing Your Inner Circle Impact

Your best chance at building momentum for others starts in your own backyard. The people you come into contact with every day— your family, friends, co-workers, and acquaintances. By focusing here, you lay the foundation for your ripples of impact to spread.

Here are some ways to drop a pebble in the pond to get things started:

- **Channel your inner Brené Brown:** Take some pointers from the queen of vulnerability, University of Houston research professor and killer storyteller Brené Brown. Communicate with your inner circle with a palpable amount of empathy and vulnerability, which will help build momentum for them.
- **Become a mentor:** Look for connections within your inner circle to offer mentorship. Take the mentorship seriously and devote time to helping them build momentum.

■ **Perform an intentional act of momentum:** Choose some-one from your inner circle, and without them asking, find a way to BUMP them forward toward their goals. This unsoli-cited act can create ripples.

Take a Moment

An Intentional Act of Kindness

Choose someone from your inner circle and schedule some time to talk with them about what their goals are. Think through how you can BUMP them forward to help them create momentum.

Expanding Your Influence

Beyond your inner circle is the indirect influence you have with the people you occasionally come into contact with throughout your connected networks. Although there is an infrequency to how often you connect with the second circle, the moments you do interact can be a powerful source of influence for creat-ing momentum.

Here are some ways to make the most out of an occasional interaction:

■ **Leave the time machine at home:** When you *do* have the opportunity to interact on occasion, be in the moment. You learned the dangers of your mind becoming a mental time machine in Chapter 1. Leave the mental time machine at home and be focused on the present moment. Avoid dis-tractions and make a genuine effort to connect.

■ **Be a connector:** Think strategically about whom you could connect someone with to help them on their journey, and make the connection. Since you don't have interactions every day, this is a fantastic way to help the occasional contact build momentum.

- **Write down the details:** During your interaction, write down the interesting details about the person. Being able to mention these details in a future interaction will create a sense of belonging and meaning. Sometimes it's remembering the small things that creates the biggest impact.

Impacting the System

Using your influence to impact the world at large can seem like dropping a pebble in the ocean. How much impact can you really have? Creating systemic change happens when we all decide to own our moments and use them to create a better world for everyone.

Here are a few ideas to help you change the world:

- **Amp up your activism:** Find organizations that are doing work that speaks to your heart and become an active supporter of their work. Go beyond wearing the cool T-shirt and really contribute through your non-negotiable values. Help them build the momentum to affect change.
- **Invest in your community:** Find ways to invest in your community with your time and money. Volunteer to help at the local homeless shelters, soup kitchens, and community centers. You can make a tangible difference in the community you live in with a little deliberate intention and a lot of heart.
- **Make better consumer choices:** Use your buying power to make a statement about what you truly care about. Buy that ethically sourced coffee, get your meat and eggs at the local farm, and speak up when you find out about questionable supply-chain issues and practices. Becoming an informed consumer helps drive a powerful message about the products and companies you want to help build momentum.

A Legacy You Can Bank on

I recently had an opportunity to keynote for the North Dakota–based Bravera Bank. Once every four years, they hold a company-wide conference to celebrate their wins and reveal the big goals they want to achieve over the next four years. Bravera is now one of North Dakota's largest banks, having experienced explosive growth over the past few years. When you experience that kind of growth, it can be easy to let the culture slide a bit in the face of expansion. But Bravera is different.

My wife and I had a chance to grab dinner with their CEO, David Ehlis, and we were really moved by his approach to leadership. Bravera focuses not just on hitting the big goals but on the holistic health of their employees. Their first focus is on their people. They maximize their influence over their inner circle by investing in the lives of the ones carrying out their mission. They promote from within whenever possible and highlight the incredible work of their team.

When my wife and I walked into the conference center, Bravera had signs all over the room featuring different employees explaining the incredible value each employee brought to the organization. To take a moment and shine a light on the individual efforts of some of their employees is incredibly thoughtful. I saw these employees posting these images on LinkedIn after the conference, proud of their efforts and the organization they work for.

It was no surprise to find that Bravera is an employee-and-director-owned company. Every employee is empowered to own their moments. They understand that the quality of service they provide to the customers who occasionally walk into their lobbies has an indirect impact on the lives of their customers' families and the communities the bank serves.

From investing in their people to contributing time and money to the local organizations they support, Bravera is building a moment-driven legacy every day.

The Power of Cumulative Impact

Sometimes, it can seem that small individual actions can't generate enough momentum to move things forward, but the cumulative impact of these actions taken by many people creates "compound momentum." Every act of empathy, every moment of mentoring, and every meaningful connection contributes to the greater good. The power is not in the magnitude of the individual moments but in the collective force of everyone doing their part to create momentum for themselves and others.

Conclusion

What will people say about *you* when you're gone?

I know this is an unsettling question, but if you look at it through the lens of momentum, it can be strangely motivating. At some point in your life, you might ask yourself, "What kind of mark am I going to leave behind?" Here is the thing: it isn't about what you leave *behind*. It's about how you empower those around you to move *forward*. Your legacy is built in the everyday moments, those tiny interactions in which you create momentum for others that can shape lives, generate hope, and drive success. That is the power of a moment-driven legacy.

You shouldn't wait until the end of your life to start thinking about legacy. You should start now. The longer the time you have to focus on capturing and creating moments of momentum, the longer your 2nd Life will be. You don't need to make grand gestures or perform heroic feats. Just don't let everyday moments slip through your fingers. Use these moments to make strong emotional connections that convince others that their circumstances are temporary and change is possible. Remember the rats! Ordinary people are capable of doing extraordinary things.

It is my hope, that is, my desire and expectation, that you found this book helpful and that it inspired you to use Moment Momentum to create powerful transformational experiences for yourself and others. My desire is for you to build unstoppable momentum. My expectation is that you will post about your moments of momentum on social media. From the tiny, relatable everyday moments, to the going viral OGRE moments. Sharing these moments can inspire others and make them believe they are capable of more. This is a powerful way to build your 2nd Life legacy and create an incredible cumulative impact. Find me online (@brantmenswar) and tag me in your moments. I can't wait to see how the momentum you create for yourself and others is crushing big goals all over the world.

Answering the question of what people will say about you when you're gone may seem like you're writing your obituary, but you are really writing your next chapter. You get to decide how much impact you can have, starting with the moments you create today. You are building a legacy, not a tombstone.

Go design a life worth remembering.

Moments to Remember:
- Your 2nd Life is how long your name will be spoken after you die.
- The length of your 2nd Life is directly proportionate to how much momentum you create for others.
- Your legacy is built in concentric circles of influence.

(continued)

(*continued*)

- Your best chance at building momentum for others starts in your own backyard.
- Systemic change happens when we all decide to own our moments and use them to create a better world for everyone.
- Every act of empathy, every moment of mentoring, and every meaningful connection contributes to the greater good.
- You shouldn't wait until the end of your life to start thinking about legacy.
- Your legacy is built in the everyday moments, those tiny interactions in which you create momentum for others, that can shape lives, generate hope, and drive success.

Acknowledgments

THIS BOOK WOULD not have been possible without the help of some incredible people. Steve Carlis, Hank Norman, Vella Petrova, Kristen Cox, Arestia Rosenberg, Maxwell Lindsay, and the rest of the 2 Market Media team, you are truly amazing! Jill Marsal and the team at Marsal Lyon Literary Agency, thank you for your belief in this book and in me. Cheryl Segura, you got "me" before I even knew what this book could be. Thank you for your trust and encouragement. Angela Morrison, you are a wonderful editor, thank you for keeping me in line. Sangeetha Suresh and the rest of the Wiley team, thank you for all your effort to bring this book to life.

My amazing group of friends, mentors, and colleagues who gave me their honest feedback even when I didn't want it. Col. Noel Zamot, your brain is what I'm missing! Ali Levine, your belief in me is unwavering, and I am so honored to call you a dear friend. Laura Gassner Otting (LGO), your star continues to rise, and I am humbled by your willingness to step up and help wherever and whenever I need it. Todd Van de Kruik, your creativity continues to blow me away. Thank you for all your input and critical thinking toward the big picture.

Senoia Coffee, Leaf and Bean, and Sharpsburg Pizza & Pub, thank you for being my "field trip" offices.

My family, thank you for bearing with me through this mad dash and keeping me sane. Brady and Miranda, I promise to not miss any more birthdays. Natalie Rose, my personal Encyclopedia Britannica for everything I ever wanted to know…and not know…thank you for lending me your rizz whenever needed. Jeffrey, you were smart to play hockey a thousand miles away and miss this chaos! My incredible wife, Sherry, none of this would have been possible without you. If any of this becomes a breakthrough success, it's because of you. I love you.

To you, the reader, thank you for saying yes to this book. I hope you decide to capture the moments in front of you and start building the 2nd Life impact that will make your legacy legendary. Just take it one moment at a time.

About the Author

BRANT MENSWAR STANDS at the forefront of corporate and personal transformation, masterfully equipping both organizations and individual trailblazers to navigate the current work landscape and ascend to new heights of performance. He is a best-selling author, is certified in the Psychology of Leadership from Cornell University, and has been named one of the country's top motivational speakers. His dynamic live events are a fusion of groundbreaking research and powerful narratives that create "moments" to remember and ignite an emotional call to action among attendees.

With more than a decade of strategic involvement with elite global brands, Brant has honed an unparalleled expertise in catalyzing connection, sparking engagement, and helping organizations achieve their big goals. He has been called "America's Personal Development Coach" having appeared on ABC, NBC, CBS, and FOX and has worked with companies like Netflix, Verizon, Hilton, Microsoft, ESPN, Sony Pictures Entertainment, and dozens more to help them create unstoppable momentum.

Index